New Times: New Families

New Times: New Families

by

Victoria Carrington
Graduate School of Education,
University of Queensland, Australia

KLUWER ACADEMIC PUBLISHERS
DORDRECHT / BOSTON / LONDON

A C.I.P. Catalogue record for this book is available from the Library of Congress.

ISBN 1-4020-0481-8

Published by Kluwer Academic Publishers,
P.O. Box 17, 3300 AA Dordrecht, The Netherlands.

Sold and distributed in North, Central and South America
by Kluwer Academic Publishers,
101 Philip Drive, Norwell, MA 02061, U.S.A.

In all other countries, sold and distributed
by Kluwer Academic Publishers,
P.O. Box 322, 3300 AH Dordrecht, The Netherlands.

Printed on acid-free paper

Printed in the Netherlands.

DEDICATION

Allan.... thank you for the knowledge.

Brook.... thank you for the joy.

TABLE OF CONTENTS

INTRODUCTION

There can be little doubt that ours is a society riding the crest of vast and profound social and economic change. The material conditions and social landscapes through which we experience our lives are increasingly an unchartered sea of unanticipated shift and hidden consequence and many of us have the unsettling feeling that we are out of our depth. It is natural to respond to this rapid and fundamental change with concern, particularly when many of the enduring keystones of our lives have been problematized. Family is one such keystone.

Family—and its apparent decline—is a topic of great interest. The breakdown of marriage and other relationships, family roles and responsibilities, the alienation of children, the rights of grandparents, juvenile crime and drug usage, and the emotional fallout of divorce are all current and emotive issues. Few individuals remain untouched by this debate.

The changes we are witnessing in relation to family are made all the more worrisome because we have a limited vocabulary for discussing and understanding profound change—a vocabulary characterized by normative framings and assumptions of deficit. It is very easy to look at the changes in 'traditional' family structure and read 'breakdown', 'decline' and 'loss'. A politics of blame and rhetoric of 'reconstitution' very quickly follows. However, given the fundamental nature of contemporary social and economic change, this is not an adequate response. The shifts that we have experienced will not disappear; there will be no reversion to the 'good old days'; and to continue to interpret change through a lens of deficit is counterproductive. We therefore need to develop a framework and vocabulary for addressing families in new times.

New Times: New Families begins the exploration of a new vocabulary and new theoretical framing that might have some salience given the context of new times. It begins by outlining how we came to talk about the modern nuclear family—what we would now call the 'traditional' family—in negative terms, chronicles some of the fundamental changes that have taken place of late, and then building upon current sociological and cultural studies work, it describes a new, more flexible framework that can accommodate difference and ongoing change without looking for lack or dysfunction.

PART ONE

CONTEXTUALIZING FAMILY

Like every proper ideology, the family too was more than a mere lie

(The Frankfurt Institute 1972, p. 138).

CHAPTER 1

RECONSTITUTING TRADITIONAL FAMILY

Partial Transcript of the Prime Minister The Hon. John Howard MP Speech at the Launch of the Family Tax Initiative, Wentworthville, Sydney. 16th December 1996.

This represents the delivery in full, on time, without subtraction, without qualification of probably the centrepiece of the policies that we took to the last election and it is true that over a long period of time I have talked a lot about the importance of policy supporting the family. I regard them as very critical to the future society that I would like Australia to have. I want to in the period that we are in Government, I want us to leave a permanent mark on the Australian community, a mark that restores and strengthens the role of the family unit within our society, a strengthening within our society that gives to parents more choice. The key to our family tax initiative is that it recognises the additional costs of bringing up children and it also seeks to give to the parents of Australia's children a lot more choice as to how they order their lives. We as a Government don't seek to impose stereotypes on Australian parents. We don't seek to tell Australian parents that when their children are young, one parent should be permanently at home while one is in the workforce but we do want to give them increasingly the option to do that if that is their choice but whether or not they do it is a matter for the choice of individual parents.

I can remember about eight or nine years ago making a speech in which I said that a taxation system that doesn't recognise the cost of raising children, a taxation system that adopts an antiseptic, economic neutrality towards the cost of raising children is a taxation system without a social vision. And this family tax initiative which will deliver one billion dollars of tax concessions to people with children, it is carefully targeted to help low and middle income families. It helps sole parent families as well as helping two parent families. We recognise the enormous struggle of many sole parents in our community and we applaud them for the contribution they make single-handedly to raising their children and although all of us in an ideal world would like to see children raised by a mother and a father, we must always recognise the massive burden that is carried by sole parents when usually through no fault of their own and against their wishes. I have never met a sole parent yet who really in an ideal world would like to be a sole parent but it happens that way, but we're not into judgemental things. We are into espousing the cause of traditional family values and espousing the importance and value if it's possible, the role model of having both a mother and a father but also recognising that in some cases, that's not possible and having a willingness to support those within our community who raise children on their own.

So we have committed ourselves in so many areas of Government policy to supporting families. I have often said that apart from the emotional value that a family brings, apart from its capacity to inculcate values from one generation to the next. Apart from the male and female role models that it provides for young children, the family also happens to be the most efficient social welfare system that any nation has ever devised and a united, fully functioning family provides the most valuable social security safety net that mankind has yet devised. So for all of those reasons I am immensely proud of what the Government has done in this area and I am immensely proud that on time, to the very last dollar and cent, without any subtraction and without any qualification, we are delivering on the commitment we made. We made that commitment, we carefully targeted it. We wanted it to be a symbol of our commitment to the role of the family in Australian society and it is but one example of the many ways in which you will find the Government that I lead, that I am very proud to lead, will always place the family at the centre of policy making considerations.

INTRODUCTION

Immanuel Wallerstein once said, "It is safest to presume that long-standing intellectual confusions are deliberate and the fact of the confusion should itself be the starting point of the analysis" (1991, p. 159). The nuclear family is a perfect example of a long-standing intellectual confusion. It has become one of the folk theories (Ogbu 1987) of modern western society, yet it is rarely seen as 'deliberate'. Perhaps it is time.

In contemporary public discourse, 'family' is represented as both the source of all social problems and their solution, generally in terms of the breakdown and then restoration of 'traditional' family values or structures. The idea of 'family' is linked directly to the prevailing political and economic climate and it is easy to think about it only in terms of decline and crisis. This is not a new phenomenon. Talcott Parsons, in the 1950s, was arguing that the family was not in decline, but instead that a new family form that suited new social and economic conditions—the nuclear family---was emerging. Ironically, contemporary conservative politics argues that the nuclear family constitutes 'traditional family' and that *it* is now under threat and in decline and, along with it, the very fabric of our society. Links are made between the breakdown of this traditional family and any number of crises from falling literacy rates through increasing single motherhood to increasing juvenile crime. What we understand by 'family' is itself contested and fluid, enmeshed within the politics of nationhood, economics and identity: the composition of 'family', and who has the power to decide what constitutes 'traditional' or acceptable, becomes an ideological battlefield as opposing perspectives manoeuvre for political and economic advantage. The stakes are high because accepted representations of nuclear family very quickly become self-evident social 'truths' transmitted via mass media and folk theories (Ogbu 1987), making these narratives difficult to dislodge. It is the constitution and reconstitution of that family that is the subject and object of this text. In order to ground the theoretical work of this text, I draw at times from the Australian experience of the last few years, particularly the ethnic and racial shift that has become part of the contemporary cultural landscape. It is, I believe, illustrative of the complexities of conceptualising family within new economies.

NEOLIBERAL RECONSTITUTION OF 'TRADITIONAL' FAMILY IN AUSTRALIA

John Howard's term as Liberal Prime Minister has been characterized by a conservative, neoliberal agenda—a commitment to minimal government intervention, pullback of social welfare from the working and middle classes, attempts to weaken trade unions and other employee representative bodies, and a belief that all social groups will ultimately benefit from the effects of corporate profit and the increasing wealth of the already-wealthy. Neoliberalism is both a political and cultural ideological position, described as the "defining political economic paradigm of our time" (McChesney 1998, p. 7). It is both political and cultural because the impacts of policies coloured by this paradigm reach far into the daily lives of individuals and groups. Depending on who and where you are, these impacts include:

> a massive increase in social and economic inequality, a marked increase in severe deprivation for the poorest nations and peoples of the world, a disastrous global environment, an unstable global economy and an unprecedented bonanza for the rich (McChesney 1998, p. 8).

In the context of this political climate, Howard (1996) has openly called for a restoration of what he identifies as the traditional family unit. He says, " I want to leave a permanent mark on the Australian community, a mark that restores and strengthens the role of the family unit"[1]. The 'traditional' family for which Howard harbours such nostalgia is the nuclear family, understood as a patriarchal mother-father-child/ren formation. This public rhetoric positions the family as the natural and neutral social unit, the family unit of "an ideal world". However, the nuclear family is anything but natural and neutral. Howard's call for a reconstitution of traditional family is, therefore, much more than simply the hope of a return to a happier time. The family of which Howard speaks does not exist unattached to an entire economic, political and social milieu and it is simply not possible to selectively recreate one or two isolated paleosymbolic traits. A government agenda to selectively 'reconstitute' such a family form must, therefore, be carefully scrutinized.

The 1996 Australian Family Tax Initiative was constructed to aid in the delivery of this restoration, as Howard's "permanent mark on the Australian community". The beginning of a new government's drive to reshape the social and economic landscape. As part of this process of strengthening the family unit Howard's government proposed a way to allow one parent to remain permanently at home. This was represented as a government offering families—nuclear families—'choice' via changes in taxation:

> We [Government] don't seek to tell Australian parents that when their children are young, one parent should be permanently at home while one is in the workforce but we do want to give them increasingly the option to do that if that is their choice.

As a precursor, changes in childcare and family payments had the result that for many parents employed in part-time or in low paying jobs—and overwhelmingly this sector of the workforce was, and remains, female—the benefit to the family of their income was lost in childcare payments and cumulative reduction of other benefits. This structural change made their 'choice' to stay out of the paid workforce

---

[1] Unless otherwise stated, John Howard is quoted from the transcript of his Family Tax Initiative Speech, 16th December, 1996.

easier. Additionally, Howard's understanding that it is women who would choose to stay at home was evident in other comments made at the time:

> I'm fed up with people attacking women who stay home to look after their children. I'm fed up with those people being treated as somehow or other they are second-class citizens (cited in Duffy 1998, p. 5).

Again, the tax restructuring was presented as a policy about choice in a free market, giving mothers the 'choice' to stay at home and look after their young children. In this, an ideological and economic agenda was shrouded in an apolitical terminology. However, as a result, many women are forced out of employment—a very political consequence.

This political move did not take place outside an economic context and without awareness of popular views of family as source and solution to perceived social crisis. The restructuring of taxation alongside a sudden concern for the reconstitution of an exclusionary model of nuclear family was patently linked to underlying neoliberal economic agendas. This agenda is, of course, not new. Margaret Thatcher, former Conservative British Prime Minister, noted a relationship between escalating welfare costs (unacceptable under neoliberal philosophy) and the decline of 'traditional family'. She argued in relation to the trend away from this family, that it "is clear that at present we are moving rapidly in the wrong direction" (1995, p. 550). Foreshadowing Howard's social agenda, and reflecting the discourse of family as cause and solution of social ailments, she suggested a clear connection between "crime, dependency and family breakdown" (p. 551). Reflecting views of the family as both source of, and solution to, social problems and taking advantage of community fear of crime and instability, Thatcher advocated the strengthening of the traditional family and argued that "if we are serious about the family as the most fundamental unit of society, that has implications for economic policy too. It should, for example, be reflected in the tax system" (p. 564). These are precisely the conservative and fiscal concerns which were at work in Australian politics.

The only other family form mentioned by Howard at this time was the 'sole parent family'. The implication was that this family was a problem, formed around lack and breakdown. In relation to single parent families, Howard states:

> we [Liberal Government] are into espousing the cause of traditional family values and espousing the importance and the value the role model of having both a mother and a father.

Single parent families are guilty of a deficit in financial capacity and in the ability to provide traditional female and male role models. They are lesser models of family. This understanding of the deficit positioning of single parent families is further clarified when he notes "but we're not into judgemental things" and argues that we need to display "a willingness to support those in our community who raise children on their own". Self perception as deficit is assumed as he notes that sole parents operate in this family form "against their wishes" and also notes that he has "never met a sole parent yet who really ... would like to be a sole parent". Any number of single parents would loudly dispute this judgement on their lives and the choices they've made. The message, however, is clear: in their state of lack, these families are a potential source of social breakdown. Significantly, other family forms did not rate a mention. 'Traditional' family becomes a narrative about mum, dad and the kids. What goes unstated is the constructed nature of this narrative (for it *is* a story) and its role in a particular type of economic and social environment.

As I have noted, implicit in the politics of this tax initiative and its rhetoric is a focus on the family as both source and solution of social ills. The breakdown of the traditional, strong heterosexual nuclear family is the source of societal fragmentation, and it is in the restoration and strengthening of this family that the solution can be found. Implicit here is a link between the restoration of the traditional nuclear family and the economic and moral health of the nation. This is not unlike the ongoing literacy crisis which has overtaken Australia—regardless of identified improvements in literacy skills, the growth in numbers of non-English speaking and English-as-a-second-language Australians in our school system, and the expansion of our expectations—we are continually told that we are in the throes of a literacy crisis which ultimately threatens the nation's productivity, standing in the international community and moral fibre. The economic benefit of traditional family is clear as Howard hints at the economic benefits of a return to nuclear families and goes on to reflect the neoliberal commitment to welfare withdrawal when he notes the "efficient social welfare system" it provides. However, what Howard unproblematically identifies as the traditional Australian family is a *narrative*, a constructed myth disseminated, in part, via the burgeoning public culture of the 1950s and 1960s.

The media family, standard fare of 1950s and 1960s, demonstrated the power and naturalness of the nuclear family and turned its narrative features into a story of perfect family life. Consider, for example, *The Honeymooners, I Love Lucy, Father Knows Best* and a host of James Stewart movies. All these hugely successful television and film productions pivoted around the workings of the patriarchal nuclear family. Just as powerfully, these shows also portrayed appropriate gender roles for the times: *Leave It To Beaver* and *The Dick Van Dyke Show* depicted women entrenched in domestic bliss and men who went to the office each day. David Dale (1998, p. 1) described the 1960s television comedy *Bewitched* as showing "that the only way a smart woman could break out of the housewife stereotype was to use magic". We could just as easily argue that she used magic to maintain the illusion of being a 'normal' housewife. Thus, magic was never quite enough to break out of the nuclear mould, nor, as Mrs. Robinson discovered in *Lost in Space,* was travelling a million light years from Earth. There were also many television shows depicting life outside the nuclear family, for example *My Three Sons* and later, *The Brady Bunch.* Yet these families were all depicted as having suffered loss of either mother or father, allowing us to measure and understand them against the nuclear template.

Teenage movies such as the *Gidget* series told us that while it was fine to play on the beach during summer, nice young girls finally found happiness in the arms and kitchen of a clean-cut young man. Mass circulation women's magazines paralleled television and film. In Australia, the most influential of these has been *The Australian Women's Weekly*. Throughout its history, the *Weekly* has celebrated the housewife and mother, giving recipe tips, home decorating ideas, and instructing on the basics of good mothering and childcare. Generations of Australian women have grown up with these textual icons and have referenced their behaviours, and those of others, against them. At the same time, men were unproblematically constructed as wage-earners and head of the household, and children were depicted in accordance with particular narratives of childhood. These prepubescent gender stereotypes, along with the nuclear narrative, have appeared throughout much of the standardized reading texts of schooling between the 1950s and the present as well as on television. These texts actively displayed appropriate behaviours for boys and girls and, at the same time, created a virtually adult-free zone, a children's universe: mothers make an appearance to take the children shopping or to deliver afternoon tea and fathers pass by on the way to and from the office. In this world, the messages about appropriate gender roles and families are as apparent as the depictions of adult-child relationships. Overwhelmingly, boys are active and inquiring while girls are the observers—boys initiate and girls respond; children and adults live in separate worlds. Throughout the various texts of mass culture, particularly the emergent mass culture of the period between the end of the Second World War and the 1970s, messages about appropriate roles and families are clear and insistent.

Depictions of traditional values such as the one presented by the current Government set up what I would argue is a false expectation that a re-creation of these family formations will construct a stable, safe and economically vibrant Australia. These representations of nuclear family and its mythic link to stability and community are directed at those individuals and groups most at risk in new economies—the aged, rural and isolated populations, the unskilled and semiskilled and welfare recipients. The same groups that suffer the most under neoliberal policies. What is always missing from calls for a restoration of traditional family is a recognition of the underlying and necessary social and political conditions that made possible the modern nuclear family and an analysis of the normative power of this narrative. Along with notions of community, gendered social roles and integrated identity, the nuclear family is premised upon the autonomous capitalist nationstate[2]. That is, the modern (now 'traditional') nuclear family sits within a particular understanding of nation and community, one that is increasingly problematic. Within this discourse, social and economic changes such as the ones we are undergoing are understood as problems; this is translated into a breakdown of traditional family and moral decay. Therefore the solution to these problems lies in the recreation of this unifying and stabilizing social unit. Note once again that within this position the family is constructed as both the source and politically neutral

---

[2]   I have purposefully omitted the hyphen whenever using the term 'nationstate' in order to represent what I believe to have been the almost total immersion of the nation and the state within each other during that phase of capitalism which I have referred to as 'nationstate capitalism'.

solution of social problems—the breakdown of 'traditional' nuclear family structure is the source, while its restoration is the solution. This simplistic representation refuses to acknowledge the multidimensional impact of globalizing capitalism on the ways in which corporations and nationstates interact in a global economy; on the ways in which identity and social reality are constructed; and, on the rapidity and complexity of these changes. Importantly, it also fails to understand the historically and culturally positioned nature of this romanticized and highly selective family form: it is small (father, mother and children); it is place-bound (single family dwelling in local community); it is culturally and racially homogeneous. Above all else, it is exclusionary when used as a model for living. Looming in the background, unacknowledged, is the question of who gets to decide what is the appropriate form for family to take in our society and what happens to those who choose not to live in this manner.

This is a book about the way that the nuclear family has become naturalized in our society. I have found myself fascinated by how this one family form amongst others has become sanctified and held up as a blueprint for a moral and successful life. This is not the definitive review of approaches to family theory. Instead, it is a map of my exploration of this phenomenon. Consequently it reflects a subjective use and juxtaposition of theory and analysis. This, then, is a non-reconstructive and non-remediatory project to understand and situate family in relation to a broader set of changes. I believe it provides a new and interesting view of the family in contemporary society and finally, a more hopeful theoretical approach. It is organized into three distinct, but connected parts. The first part historically and economically contextualizes key approaches to analysing the 'modern' western family. It overviews the evolution of approaches to analysing family, and argues that their particular genealogies have created and maintained the mythic nuclear family. More importantly, the various developments have resulted in a limited capacity for framing the increasing fluidity of notions of 'family' or, for that matter, recognizing the highly politicized positioning of family as both source and solution of social instability. As a result, our discussion and analyses of family have been limited by a vocabulary of deficit or dysfunction. Further, these literatures are unable to link macro sociological and economic shifts, and here I refer particularly to the powerful and rapid emergence of discourses and practices of globalization, with actual empirical changes in the experience of the family. Examples from current research focusing on contemporary interethnicity in Australia[3] will be used to argue that these families are well placed as markers of these changes. Any theorization which is to claim relevance for new times must be able to position families of difference, whether this difference be cultural, racial or sexual, without recourse to terminologies of lack or misfortune.

---

[3] This data is drawn from the *Interethnic Families* project, a three-year (1996-1998) qualitative study funded by the Australian Research Council. The principal investigators are C. Luke and A. Luke from the University of Queensland. The Project Coordinator is V. Carrington. In this research, 'interethnicity' is used to describe families that are cross-racial and cross-cultural.

To accomplish this I bring together a number of literature bases which do not normally speak to one another. I make use of critiques of the existing order by Deleuze and Guattari (1983, 1987), Deleuze (1997), Wilden (1980, 1987) and Bourdieu (1977a, 1977b, 1977c, 1984, 1990, 1991, 1994) in order to dissect the politicized and libidinous 'family' which is obscured by, and yet foundational to, traditional theorizations. The nuclear family is revealed as a highly politicized social form and its status as a normative narrative is linked to a specific set of economic conditions. Deleuze and Guattari, in particular, hint at the increasing fluidity of experience and self within capitalism, arguing the interconnectedness of the social being with the demands of an emergent "capitalist axiomatic". However, their writing in the late 1960s and 1970s predates the accelerated shift into globalization that we have since experienced.

In the second section, I explore the evolution of capitalism that has occurred after these critiques were developed. In particular, I focus here on the shift out of Fordist capitalism—what I refer to as 'nationstate' capitalism—into what Deleuze and Guattari (1983) referred to as the "capitalist axiomatic". I make this move because I am convinced, as were Deleuze and Guattari, Marcuse and others, that the ways in which we construct ourselves and our social worlds are intricately tied to the forms of capitalism in which we are immersed. I make no apology for the strong connection I make between the prevailing phase of capitalism and the type of society in which we live and the ways in which we are constructed to view and experience this society. In my view, these things are so entwined as to be inseparable. To understand contemporary social life we need to frame it within the forms of capitalism in which it is enmeshed. Returning to the notion of ethnicity as a grounding instrument, I argue that constructions of ethnicity have been linked to the ideological requirements of the nationstate and, as such, are increasingly fragmented and strategic in the shift into globalizing capitalism.

In the final section, I take the essence of these previous two sections and interrogate the implications of globalization for nationstate, community and the family. I pick up the changing and contested role of ethnicity in new times. Following this, and making the link back to family, in this Chapter, I introduce the experiences of interethnic families in Australia to argue that there is a qualitatively different form of family emergent from the flows of globalizing capitalism. This family, I will argue, is increasingly tied to the normative agendas of the capitalist axiomatic rather than the Fordist nationstate. I begin, then, to trace out what these emerging processes of symbolic violence might look like and, on the basis of this, suggest the broad parameters of a new conceptualization of 'family' in new times.

Barrett and McIntosh (1991) note retrospectively that in their feminist text, *The Anti-Social Family,* they displayed a particular unacknowledged ethnocentrism. They write:

> While there is a long and honourable tradition in feminism of producing theory from
> our own experience and of political action in whatever patch we find ourselves, it

nevertheless was and is clearly not legitimate for white women to write as if those experiences are universal or that patch the whole field of struggle (pp. 164-165).

So, we come to my position in this text. Like, Barrett and McIntosh, I am a white woman. I am a middle class, white female academic. I grew up within the framework of a family where my mother struggled against the normative expectations of the nuclear narrative. At the peak of her working life as a teacher she found herself 'put off' every holiday period and rehired at the start of each new school term. Every year, this amounted to at least ten weeks without an income and, ultimately, a career of itinerant teaching. There was no access to supervised and accredited childcare for her young children—she was forced to trust a series of elderly ladies and relatives. There was no government funding to assist her to meet the expense of this 'backyard' childcare, instead, full costs had to be paid entirely from her income—an income which was considerably less that that of a male doing the same job. Because she was not a permanent employee, her access to promotion was negligible, and many of the work-related benefits my generation takes as a right were the sole preserve of males. For my mother and her generation, just keeping a job was supposedly reward enough. This treatment, not just of my mother, but of an entire generation, was premised on the view that theirs was a secondary income, a lesser career. Throughout this period, my mother endured, as well, the jibes and pursed lips of an older generation of family members who believed her to be a difficult and selfish woman who should have been satisfied to look after her husband and children

This legacy of selfishness and 'abnormality' has been transferred to my own life. My own attempt at creating the white, monocultural nuclear family was spectacularly ill fated. In the fall-out of the dissolution of my own marriage, I too have been constructed as difficult and a sub-optimal mother by various extended family members and acquaintances. Much of this has been linked to expectations of appropriate behaviour, roles and the pre-eminence of the nuclear family. This is not, and never could be, a neutral exploration of family. I am a woman and therefore cannot speak to the experiences of males in a hegemonic society or patriarchal family formation. I have also experienced the break-down of the dream and the guilt and blame that is often associated with it. Driven partly by my recollections of my mother's experience, partly by my own unfortunate family experience, and partly by my own theoretical interest in the processes of symbolic violence which construct us as social beings, I have chosen to write about the normative agenda of the traditional nuclear family. These experiences have given me cause to stop and reflect. This book is a reflection of this process. As well, this is, of course, a white western narrative. In many ways this representation of family excludes the experiences of women and men who are not white, who have differing cultural practices and values systems. I cannot claim a knowledge of these forms of life nor share their experiences. However, I have constructed a critique of this normative narrative, arguing that not only did it constrain and construct particular subjectivities within a particular moment in capitalism, but it also purposefully acted to exclude—to withhold recognition and inclusion from vast numbers of men, women and children.

It is this recognition that has led me to focus on interethnicity as a marker of family shift in our society. This understanding has allowed me to reconceptualize family in new times, a framing which I hope does not hinge on the violence of sexual or racial exclusion. Thus I do not address issues of appropriate family function and boundaries. Nor do I examine the family as a site of emotional support or site of child-rearing[4]. I do not attempt to invalidate the reality of nuclear family as a lived experience. What I attempt is to capture and represent theoretically the fluidity of family in changing times.

---

[4]   Barrett and McIntosh (1991) provide an excellent discussion of these aspects of family.

CHAPTER 2

APOLITICAL ACCOUNTS OF THE FAMILY

INTRODUCTION

This Chapter is both historical and observational, setting out a cross section of major approaches to understanding and theorizing 'family' in contemporary society. My interest lies in identifying the unarticulated presumptions of form and function of 'family' underpinning these major framings, presumptions which flow into institutional and public discourses. Interestingly, when the key approaches to conceptualising family are set out, it is possible to identify a division in the way 'family' is understood. This can profitably be conceptualized as a division between *apolitical* and *politicized* understandings of family. *Apolitical* approaches are those that represent the nuclear family as natural and universal. Rather than developing an analysis of the ideological and political contexts in which various family forms occur and operate, these accounts choose to represent the family as an apolitical site. Some reference themselves to God, others to the natural evolutionary progress of human societies, while the more recent make use of the terminologies and understandings of psychology and psychoanalysis. Generally speaking, these are approaches characteristic of the 1940s through the early 1970s, situated solidly in the economic, political and social phase of Fordist capitalism. By contrast, *politicized* approaches to conceptualising family assume that the family is a site of political manipulation and exploitation. While tempting, it is important not to imagine a linear progression from apolitical to politicized positionings of family. Many of them existed—and exist—contemporaneously. These diverse approaches coexist and intersect in various ways with other historical currents and with each other and to represent them in isolation is merely an analytic mechanism directed at identifying key aspects of each.

Historical positioning

The period between the two World Wars saw the disciplines of psychoanalysis and psychology gain credence, attracting both researchers and clientele. At the same time, methodology became increasingly 'scientific' and unreflectively objectivist, paving the way for a paradigmatic division between qualitative and quantitative methodologies. In this climate, the relevance of psychologically-based approaches to human behaviour which emphasised empirical and observable data was established, reflecting the hegemony of Modernist realities. As a consequence, the interwar period was dominated by the Modernist perspectives of Freud and by the social psychology of The Chicago School[5]. At the same time, the theorists of The Frankfurt School were developing a critical philosophical project questioning many of the inherent presumptions of Modernist theories of individual and social development. Their work pre and post-World War Two represents one of the key politicized understandings of family and will be revisited in the next Chapter. This movement towards more 'scientific' and individualized approaches to the family gained momentum in the post-World War Two period—a time characterized by an emergent US technological and cultural hegemony. These newer approaches did not replace already existing dialogues about the family. They were added to the simmering pot of research, theorizing, moralizing and exploitation that became associated with the family.

America had not been under direct threat during this war and emerged in a stronger economic position than when it began its campaign. Assuming what it now believed to be its rightful place in the world, the United State was the driving force behind the Bretton-Woods agreements which established international economic institutions such as the World Bank and the International Monetary Fund, set the US dollar to a fixed price of gold, and which outlined a set of global economic principles. As well it was the architect of The United Nations Charter and of collective security systems such as NATO and ANZUS which, according to Clark (1997), "constituted an interlocking network of security arrangements extending across much of the globe" (p. 133). The United States unrelentingly used its post-war economic power to secure its geopolitical agenda as the Cold War unfolded and was played out. It took its role in international relations, and itself, very seriously. The Cold War world was a place of tension and global insecurity as the new world order slowly took shape. Internally, there was a perceived need to construct a strong American social and moral order in order to maintain economic, spiritual and technological advantage over the Soviet Union and the threat of communism. Enter the need to establish and maintain the strong, durable nuclear family.

Mirroring the Modernist vision of a victorious America, the social sciences experienced the emergence of a systematic theory development approach increasingly focussed on the creation of accurate and valid systems of measurement. This approach developed an appetite for the empirical data and verifiable results characteristic of psychology and other cognitive sciences, results that are visible and easily interpreted by governments and other would-be clientele. As a consequence, new measurement techniques and new methodologies were developed which effectively shifted the research focus to the individual. In this climate, the family became a site for investigation rather than a site of investigation and since this time the family has been increasingly seen as the social site in which individual

---

[5]   What became known as The Chicago School of Sociology was one part of the collaborative social science research agenda founded by the University of Chicago in the early years of the twentieth century. The emphasis of this school was on the accumulation of first-hand empirical data—a move away from social philosophy, historical investigation and general theory (Bulmer 1984). It represented the first collective American sociological project (Bulmer 1984) and its impact is still felt today, particularly in applied social analysis of urbanization, poverty and the welfare state.

personalities are formed. Common to these approaches was a movement towards 'scientifically-based' analyses, increasingly premised upon sophisticated measurement procedures and controlled sites and carried out by 'experts'. Reflecting the concerns of psychiatry and psychology individual function and malfunction was the core concern and the family was allowed to become the required context for the development of well-formed individuals who, in turn, contributed to a moral and strong society. In this rush to measure and ideologically valorize, political analyses of the family were sidelined. At the same time, and as part of the same process, the nuclear family narrative would increasingly became a normative principle against which behaviour—both individual and group—could be measured. It was in this climate that apolitical approaches such as Structural Functionalism and Systems Theory flourished. This is the historical context in which these approaches developed and they should be understood accordingly. Evolutionary theory contributed in no small way to this climate—the constructions of linear development at its base impacted on studies of human life, contextualizing our views of individual and society.

SOCIAL DARWINISM

Social Darwinism legitimates the proposal that the modern nuclear family is the inevitable outcome of progressively more sophisticated human organisms and social organization. By this account, this evolution has taken millennia, moving humanity from Pre-Hominid to Modern social and cultural organizations. Fundamental to this view were presumptions of linearity—the notion of developmental stages through which human society and the family form have moved, from early primate-like groupings characterized by sexual promiscuity, through group marriage, polygamy, and finally the development of modern monogamous marriage and the nuclear family (Engels 1972; Morgan 1963).

What took shape within these framings of progress was a seemingly self-evident biological and social human hierarchy. The developmental continuum constructed within this hierarchy reinforced a polemic between primitive and modern societies which became the 'us' of sociology and the 'them' of anthropology. Although this dichotomy has been challenged (Goody 1971, 1983), there has continued to be a disciplinary divide between an anthropological focus on primitive, traditional cultures and an attendance by sociology to modernity, and ostensibly progressive societies. What are *different* social systems are perceived, via this dualist epistemology, as equal, and consequently available for scrutiny, comparison and measurement (see, for example, Parsons 1977; Zelditch 1955). This symmetrization of relations renders ideologically imposed valuations such as the equation of modernity with a higher degree of social, cultural and even intellectual development invisible. This allows the establishment of a set of us/them, modern/primitive value judgements which are taken to be value-neutral. They are, however, in no way neutral. Their equation of nuclear family with an evolutionary highpoint requires a particular interpretation of difference—one that positions non-Western, nonindustrial social formations against Western societies and judges them according to a system which has already decided that modern, industrialized societies represent a higher point of development along a linear scale. The Eurocentrism and racial stereotyping of such a scaffold is obvious. While Hegel and Marx understood capitalist society to be the outcome of a lengthy and convoluted evolutionary process, they and others paid scant attention to the accompanying construction of the white, nuclear family as the highpoint of human social development. This effectively rendered other social, racial and cultural organizations inferior. Interestingly, the Christian religion underwrites the legitimacy of this representation via depictions of the prototypal nuclear family centered around Christ, his virgin mother, Mary, and her partner, Joseph. This family is almost universally depicted as European, which is unusual given that the biblical stories are set in the Middle East. Race and culture have been neatly subsumed within the larger narrative of family. This narrative constitutes a code, a discursive construction that underwrites recent Western assumptions about the universality and appropriateness of the nuclear family form and the patriarchal social system upon which it is ultimately based.

The equation of nuclear family with moral certitude and progress is one outcome of the binarism which has characterized modern western thought. These essential dualisms draw upon the western turn to rationality dating from the seventeenth century nominal separation of Church and State, mind and body[6]. From this point, Western philosophy and science took as its core proposition the separation of reality into a series of oppositions, for example, man/woman, individual/society, life/death, and the mind/body separation which made the capitalist alienated labor relationship possible (Wilden 1980). This categorization of human experience in terms of oppositions has remained at the core of Western constructions of reality to the present. What is particularly interesting is that these fundamental changes in the way we perceived ourselves, our god and our nation coincided with the emergence of capitalism as an identifiable mode of economic practice.

Goody (1996) suggests that the highly influential polarity between family (nuclear) and kinship (extended) developed within structural anthropology is of a kind with the opposition set up between individual and society, East and West, primitive and modern. What Goody describes as "concealed judgements that tend to distort what we are doing and thinking" (p. 163) have allowed the West to construct a narrative, focussed on the nuclear family and its links to industrialization, to justify its belief in its own uniqueness. The ideological, rather than essential, character of this narrative can be easily established. Goody (1996) problematizes assumptions that the nuclear family is a prerequisite for industrialization. As an illustration, he traces the development of industrialization in India within the framework of the extended family, and further, points to the existence and operation of extended family connections in Western industrial and capitalist societies (Goode 1963, 1971; Young & Willmott 1962, 1973). His argument for the continued existence of extended

---

6   Anthony Wilden provides a particularly relevant overview of this process and its relationship to capitalism in *System and Structure* (1980).

family networks in industrialized societies updates Goode's (1963) argument that, while unproductive in an economic context which rewards nuclear families, extended family connections did not automatically disappear with the advent of industrialization. Laslett's (1972) historical study of family size in Britain and the United States, among a number of nations, also refuted any causal relationship between family size and industrialization, and, in fact, identified nuclear families in the pre-industrial history of Europe.

The point here is that the size and shape of post-industrial western family configurations is not unique. Nor is it, per se, a prerequisite for industrialization. Regardless, the nuclear family has, since the mid-twentieth century, been constructed as the natural social form in western epistemology and has informed much of the theorizing of family in the West. In a justification of these unproblematic presumptions of increasing complexity and sophistication, early Western sociologies took the view that the process of industrialization acted to undermine the extended family, mitigating instead for the formation of smaller, nuclear family units. Modern, Western societies, by this account, were once based on extended family relationships, but the shift to industrialization and progress along the one-way evolutionary continuum has resulted in the emergence of the nuclear family. It is here that the seeming naturalness of the nuclear family and its connection to modern life begins to emerge, reinforced by references to evolutionary theory and structural anthropology. It has become a normative narrative against which others, and ourselves, have been measured. Via a series of reinforcing moral and scientistic steps, the extended family has been stereotyped, coloured, and directly associated with the East and pre-industrial (read 'remedial') societies. Against this, the Western, white nuclear family has been associated with industrialization and progress. And, these particular formations have been represented as opposite poles along a continuum of family formations that range from prehistoric kinships groupings through to modern nuclear families.

It cannot be mere coincidence that a colour spectrum running from darkest to lightest corresponded with this developmental continuum. Hidden within this structured history of social development was a colour-coding system overlaid with spurious connections between race and cultural practice. Thus, not only was social progress linear, moving humans from primitive, 'traditional' cultures to sophisticated, 'modern' societies, but it was accompanied by a connection between evolutionary status and colour (Vidich & Lyman 1994). That is, colour, or race, was taken to be an indicator of position along the primitive-modern continuum established within these nominally apolitical sociological and anthropological perspectives. Stratton suggests that:

> by the late nineteenth century a combination of scientific racism and social Darwinism, which had served to legitimate plantation slavery and colonisation, had led to a privileging of race as the key determinant in the hierarchical distinctions between people (1998, p. 49).

This colour-coding was extended to assertions that different races had differing thought processes (Levy-Bruhl 1975) and sexual mores (Mead 1943, 1961), and further, could be arranged in a hierarchy of intelligence (Herrnstein & Murray 1994). Thus, by associating colour, and hence race, with a particular position along the developmental continuum, non-white individuals and groups were constructed as innately deficit—culturally, morally and intellectually. The modern West, then, created a version of reality which established the nuclear family as its characteristic social formation, against which it could measure other societies. Additionally, it constituted a moral order, representing appropriate social forms and activities, premised on an equation of modern family with homogeneous white nuclear families. This becomes a powerful normative agenda. Important here is recognition that the West has framed and understood the nuclear family cannot be separated from the processes of capitalism or from ideological agendas such as Christian dogma, scientific theory or notions of nation.

What is fascinating is the way in which this family narrative, and the normative agenda it constitutes have been represented as a natural outcome of human social evolution. This is the fundamental, and implicit, understanding of apolitical approaches to the family—that the nuclear family is simply the pattern in which humans in modern societies, if left to follow their natural inclinations, will choose to live. This is a misrepresentation. Views such as this fail to acknowledge the pivotal position of the nuclear narrative within a number of intersecting and overlapping ideological and political currents that together constitute Western society. Indeed, the normative principles underpinning this unit form the axis of Western modes of thought and economic activity. Much of the legitimacy for this claim has come from the work of post-war Structural Functionalist sociologists, the most influential of whom was Talcott Parsons

STRUCTURAL FUNCTIONALISM AND THE NUCLEAR FAMILY

Structural Functionalism argued that consciousness is shaped by the needs of society, and thus the social order becomes an amalgam of shared consciousness—common values and beliefs. This emphasis on morality, on common values and consensus, was fundamental to, and resounded throughout, the Structural Functionalism of Talcott Parsons (1902-1975). Parsons' sociology drew heavily upon the social psychology of George Mead, thus it is useful to briefly outline the key aspects of Mean's project. Mead (1863-1931) was part of what became known as The Chicago School, home of the new school of philosophy known as Pragmatism. For Mead, any separation or opposition of individual and society demonstrated a patent misunderstanding of the interdependent relationship between them. Searching for a middle ground conjoining individual and society, Mead argued that:

> The organization of social attitudes constituting the structure and content of the human individual self is effected both in terms of the organization of neural elements and their interconnections in the individual's nervous system, and in terms of the general ordered pattern of social or group behavior or conduct in which the individual—as a member of

the society of group of individuals carrying on that behavior—is involved (1934a, p. 238).

For Mead, the key to human social life was the existence of 'self', or rather, consciousness of self. Unlike Freud, Mead understood that self was a social, rather than biologically innate device (Miller 1973), and thus unable to exist outside its relationships with others. His theoretical project was, consequently, an investigation of the link between physiology, cognition, and the social self.

Miller writes of Mead's project that, "each self, according to Mead, develops to the extent that it can incorporate the attitudes of others in an ever-widening community of selves" (1973, p. xxii). In order to understand this relationship, Mead turned to the analysis of symbols and symbolic systems, particularly language. He was particularly concerned to demonstrate that the ability to use symbolic systems differentiated human social formations from the instinctual herd or social behaviours of other species. It was his position that:

> Symbols stand for the meanings of those things or objects which have meanings; they are given portions of experience which point to, indicate, or represent other portions of experience not directly present or given at the time when, and in the situation in which, any one of them is thus present (or is immediately experienced). The symbol is thus more than a mere substitute stimulus—more than a mere stimulus for a conditioned response or reflex.... Conditioned reflexes plus consciousness of the attitudes and meanings they involve are what constitute language, and hence lay the basis, or comprise the mechanism for, thought and intelligent conduct. Language is the means whereby individuals can indicate to one another what their responses to objects will be, and hence what the meanings of objects are; it is not a mere system of conditioned reflexes (Mead 1934a, p. 122n).

Thus, the meaning of any symbol is linked directly to the response it elicits within a social context. Here, the importance of shared symbolic systems begins to emerge, as well as the connection between symbols and behavioural function.

Crucial to this approach was the understanding that negotiated and shared symbols are the foundation of social realities and the behaviours and interactions of individual actors within these realities. According to Strauss (1934, p. xiii), "every group develops its own system of significant symbols which are held in common by its members and around which group activities are organized". Human social interactions are thus directed by interpretations of the ways in which events or objects are defined by symbols. As a result, cooperative social activity can exist only within the context of shared symbol systems. These common frameworks are constructed via role taking, where an individual develops a sense of self by imagining herself in the place of those with whom she interacts. For Mead, this internalization of a sense of the 'generalized other' was crucial:

> The principle which I have suggested as basic to human social organization is that of communication involving participation in the other. This requires the appearance of the other in the self, the identification of the other with the self, the reaching of self-consciousness through the other (Mead 1934a, p. 253).

It is only via the development of the 'generalized other' and 'generalized social attitudes'—which Mead linked to the development of 'self' (1934b, p. 261)—that the community could be organized. That is, particular ways of acting elicit particular responses, regardless of the individuals involved, so long as each shares in the same systems of values and beliefs. It is a short step from this to the emphasis on roles in Parson's sociology. Mead was interested in society in its entirety rather than in families per se. It was not until Parsons began to adapt social psychology to the emerging discipline of sociology that the focus shifted to the relationship between individual and family on one level, and between family and society on another, reconfiguring Mead's interest in the connection between individual and society and contributing to the elevation of the post-World War Two nuclear family to paleosymbolic status.

Writing in the America of the 1950s and 1960s—a society entrenched within Fordist industrial capitalism and Cold War machinations—Parsons strongly promoted the view that the isolated nuclear family was the fundamental social structure of industrialized, modern society. Parsons believed that the nuclear family he identified in post-war America was a newly emerging form of family. Rather than representing a decline in the traditional family, the nuclear family was in fact:

> a new type of family structure in a new relation to a general social structure, one in which the family is more specialized than before, but not in any general sense less important, because the society is dependent more exclusively on it for the performance of certain of its vital functions (1955 pp. 9-10).

Parsons was describing what he saw as an emergent trend in American society, a trend he linked to the requirements of modern society. He noted that the nuclear family constituted "a more specialized agency than before, probably more specialized than it had been in any previously known society" (1955, p. 9). The emphasis on role acquisition and differentiation was Parson's theoretical response to this increasing specialization.

Parsons did not perceive any connection between the family and larger political processes. This family, then, was theoretically depoliticized. While noting the individuals of a healthy family had connections to other social systems—the most crucial of which were those related to the male's occupational role (Parsons 1955, p. 19)—Structural Functionalism nevertheless viewed family to be unconnected to ideology or systems of political power. On this 'macroscopic' level, Parsons' nuclear family was almost completely functionless:

> It does not itself, except here and there, engage in much economic production; it is not a significant unit in the political power system; it is not a major direct agency of integration of the larger society. Its individual members participate in all these functions, but they do so 'as individuals' not in their role as family members (1955, p. 16).

Thus, Parsons' Structural Functionalism did not perceive the nuclear family to be a rigidly closed system, but rather a highly differentiated system—this family was highly differentiated from other social structures and had no particular relationship with them. Individuals came and went from the family to participate in social and economic life, thus the nuclear family became almost a mythic safe-haven—a neutral safety zone.

The power and significance of the nuclear family in relation to larger social structures did not escape the Structural Functionalists, however they did not see this significance in terms of the family unit, rather, it was the stabilized and normalized personalities of individuals from nuclear families that had significance. Understanding the family as a social system, a subset of the larger society, Parsons' contemporary, Zelditch (1955, p. 312), argued that:

> the system must differentiate behaviors and attitudes in order to continue to exist as a system; and that a further condition of stability is also that some specialization occur in responsibility for the attitudes and behaviors involved. It is the differentiated and structured gender roles which stabilize the nuclear family, and beyond this particular social system, the larger society.

Strict role differentiation and its close association with gender was crucial to a stable society. Role allocations and differentiations themselves were not submitted to scrutiny. Thus, while the Structural Functionalists of the 1950s, 1960s and 1970s argued quite clearly that the nuclear family was the primary unit of a stable, healthy society, they did not provide analyses of the creation of roles or their impact on individuals and the broader society. The function of this family was directed primarily at the stabilization of personality. This, in turn, led to a stable community and nation. For Parsons, the nuclear family fulfilled two core functions--the primary socialization of children and the stabilization of adult personality (1955). Both functions build upon understandings of human development drawn from psychoanalysis, particularly Freud's notions of psychosexual development, and from psychological framings of child and personality development.

In as much as the nuclear family was pre-eminently associated with the socialization and psychological development of children, Structural Functionalism views parents as a "leadership coalition" (Bales & Parsons, 1955, p. vii). Two adult role models— mother and father—are identified as crucial to the personality stabilization and maturation of children. The mother, following her initial close physical relationship with each child becomes "the focus of warmth and stability"; the father role involves material support but also "certain discipline and control functions" (Zelditch 1955, p. 314). Ineffective parental roles, described in terms of weak fathers or cold mothers, rendered this family susceptible to various 'pathologies'—deficits or anti-social behaviours. Thus, 'normal' fathers were strong male role models who provided economically and oversaw discipline while 'normal' mothers were warm, centred and provided a stable home and emotional life. These became powerful normative models legitimated via an apolitical discourse which represented them as an essential human essence. And, while these are undoubtedly admirable qualities, their assignation on the basis of sex, and categorization of dysfunction in their absence is problematic at best.

The male role also acted to bridge occupation and the family in this schema: family status derives from the male's occupation, and his involvement with interests separate from the home maintains links with other aspects of the larger society—the 'public'. The female role is centered on wife and home-manager—the 'private'. Drawing upon labor force statistics of the late 1940s, Parsons reflects the parameters of the feminine role relative to that of the male (1955, p. 15n):

> the distribution of women in the labor force clearly confirms this general view of the balance of the sex roles. Thus, on higher levels typical feminine occupation are those of teacher, social worker, nurse, private secretary and entertainer. Such roles tend to have a prominent expressive component, and often to be "support" to masculine roles. Within the occupational organization they are analogous to the wife-mother role in the family. It is much less common to find women in the "top executive" roles and the more specialized and "impersonal" technical roles. Even within professions we find comparable differentiation, e.g., in medicine women are more heavily concentrated in the two branches of paediatrics and psychiatry, while there are few women surgeons.

Women, on the basis of sexual typing, are associated with a range of gendered characteristics. Women's roles throughout society, at all levels, are seen in relation to a set of prescriptive boundaries and always subordinate to and supportive of, the male role. By this account, two parents are necessary in order to offer "a stable focus of integration" (Zelditch 1955, p. 312). That is, to maintain a healthy balance. That these parents are male and female is made obvious in Parsons', now classic, comments on homosexuality:

> put very generally, homosexuality is a mode of structuring of human relationships which is radically in conflict with the place of the nuclear family in the social structure and in the socialization of the child. Its nearly universal prohibition is a direct consequence of the 'geometry' of family structure (1955, p. 103).

Here, homosexuality is not depicted as either criminal or immoral, but instead, as an inefficient, deviant form of relationship. Homosexuality does not provide a balanced role model nor can it provide the complementarity of roles characteristic of a heterosexual nuclear family—an alleged cross-cultural consensus is used to justify a particular moral and ideological view. On this basis, homosexuality must be minimised—inefficiency and inappropriate socialization threatens social stability. According to Parsons, a lack of appropriate gender roles destabilizes the finely balanced social system which Structural Functionalism identified as the core of a stable society. Following Freud, Parsons understood there to be an unproblematic connection between reproductive organs on the one hand and sexuality and social role on the other. He made a sure link between male sexual organs and the social role of wage earner and head of household. In the same way, he connected female sex organs with the role of homemaker. Parsons' (1955) sociology of the family moved the nuclear family away from a biological unit to a coalition of roles, however these roles were directly connected to unproblematic associations of gender with biology. For Parsons, as for Freud (1972), biology was fate: male and female roles are cast along axes of instrumentality and expressiveness with females tending towards expressiveness and males towards instrumentality. In fact, this kind of differentiation of individual roles according to gender and sexuality was understood as a marker of progressive, modern societies (Parsons 1977; Zelditch 1955).

In this way, Structural Functionalism constituted an equilibrium model focused on mutually reinforcing and stable relationships and roles (Leys 1996). That this understanding of identity and social role consistently overlaid sexual categories with gender expectations went unremarked. The nuclear family was situated at the core of these role differentiations and specializations based upon sexual, taken as gender, characteristics. Somewhere here the nuclear family moved from being a particular family shape to becoming a prescriptive recipe for living. That this particular set of rules, rather than another, formed into a normative narrative served sets of interests that Structural Functionalism was unable to describe. Implicit in this perspective was an unproblematic belief in a model of social evolution extending from primitive societies to the modern (American) system. In this view the nuclear family represented a sophisticated social formation in tune with the state of social evolution, the specialized labor requirements of industrial society and the Functionalist requirement for stability. Such a family, consisting of biological parents who fulfilled specialized male and female roles, and their immediate offspring was mobile, streamlined and internally independent. Theorizations of this family as unconnected to macroscopic processes sought to represent the nuclear family as somehow insulated from political and economic currents. Thus, the Functionalist framing was itself the product of political and economic environments, a normative framework linked to an ideological portrayal of society.

The Functionalist nuclear family has not been without its critics. As early as 1960, social anthropologist R.N. Adams argued that this theorization conflated what may be the basic requisites for a society, or the basic functions, with those of the nuclear family. Adams was unconvinced that the nuclear family formed an essential and irreplaceable component of a stable, modern society—in his view it had not been demonstrated that another social formation might not fulfil this function just as effectively. In essence, this amounted to a critique of the fundamental assumptions of Structural Functionalism—the link between nuclear family and stable modern society. The experience of industrialization in India (Goody 1996) without a social organization based on the nuclear family would seemingly add weight to Adam's earlier critique. Critics further argued that the world is far from the harmonious, homogeneous and stable system represented in this perspective. Rather, social reality is the site of cultural and social diversity where the individual and family are mired in intersecting and competing power matrices. While Structural Functionalism acknowledged that healthy family groups had connections to other social systems, it nevertheless positioned this family as a private space outside the political, economic and ideological environment. The Functionalist punctuation of society as fundamentally harmonious and complete, formed by familial, sexed building blocks, created a model of social equilibrium that denied the dynamic nature of complex systems (see Wilden 1980).

This rigidly normalized social configuration had no place for an incorporative theorization of dysfunction or an ideological tolerance for diversity, either group or individual. Racial and cultural diversity were not accounted for. Recognition of the validity of family forms other than the normative white father-mother-child triangle would undermine the ideological vision of a strong common culture standing firm against external threat, remembering here that this was a time of Cold War tensions and ideological confrontation. The institutionalization of the nuclear family becomes, in this analysis, a move in the establishment of a particular cultural and ideological hegemony—the drawing of an exclusionary boundary in terms of which groups and individuals could be both regulated and measured. Within a Functionalist model, internal family dysfunction is attributed to particular family members, rather than to the family itself (Vogel & Bell 1968). In this framing, individual characteristics are perceived as the private property of each atomised individual (Thompson & Walker 1995) rather than as a bricolage of social influences and processes which are inscribed into the habitus over time. In a reflection of the Modernist social valuation of private property—the individual is self-possessed and unitary.

Representations of neutrality aside, Functionalist theorizations of the nuclear family cannot be separated from the economic and political configurations which produced them. This 'family' was entwined with the global military, cultural and economic pre-eminence of the West. Underwriting the Functionalist view of the family was the cultural and technological hegemony of the United States within a particular phase of capitalism and an unproblematically patriarchal perspective (Haralambos 1980; Sarantakos 1996). Vidich and Lyman (1994) remind us that Parsons was writing during the Cold War decades, and contributed to the positioning of the Soviet Union and 'underdeveloped' nations as 'other' (p. 29). The modern nuclear family was, then, a weapon in the ideological battles of the 1950s and 1960s, a highly masculinized place to be. The narrativized family was middle class, white and increasingly urban, reflecting a theorization which accommodated only homogeneity, and which remained outside intersections of race, gender and class (see Morgan 1975, especially p. 42). Accordingly, the shared values of the cultural majority (the homogeneously white and middle class) were paramount and the flouting of these norms identified deviance. There was no space for the other within—the nonwhite, the poor, the ill or infirm—those individuals and groups precluded from ideologically driven stereotypic visions of an industrially advanced nation. It would be fair to say that this society demanded a heavy price for social stability. The price paid by women became the particular interest of Feminist theory, to which I will return.

SYSTEMS THEORY

Out of the years immediately following World War Two came a completely new approach to scientific investigation—Systems Theory—that for many held out the promise of a revolution in the social sciences, a scientific framework which could be applied successfully to social systems research. This paradigm brought with it an entirely new vocabulary—open systems, morphostasis and morphogenesis, feedback and redundancy—which was eagerly adopted by many. In its application to studies of the family, Systems Theory took on a cybernetic profile (Callan & Noller 1987; Noller & Fitzpatrick 1993; Sarantakos 1996) rapidly appropriated by the psychological disciplines, beginning with its incorporation of the genetic structuralism of Piaget.

Systems Theory has had its greatest impact on the field of family therapy where it has been blended into existing psychological and remediatory approaches. The development of a systems approach has made possible family therapy's focus on treating an entire family rather than the individual (Becvar & Becvar 1993; Callan & Noller 1987; Mikesell, Lusterman & McDaniel 1995). Essentially, the emphasis on normal individual functioning has been extended to include the family, marking a fundamental shift from Structural Functionalism's focus on individual dysfunction as the cause of family pathology. With this, the family was opened to professional intervention and gate keeping (Gilding 1997; Reiger 1985). The central concepts of a Systems Theory inspired perspective on the family—for example, nonsummativity; circular causality; equifinality; morphogenesis; homeostasis; communication—have been used as a springboard for the identification of family rules (Noller & Fitzpatrick 1993; Sarantakos 1996). That is, the patterns of normal functioning characteristic of 'healthy' families. In line with the claims to scientism made by Systems Theory, there is an emphasis on positive and negative feedback and processes of morphogenesis and homeostasis. This means that the self-regulation and stability of the system are under analysis rather than the interconnections between family systems and broader social dynamics within capitalism.

Families are viewed, in this approach, "as a system of interrelated parts, organised in terms of interconnecting relationships and feedback that flows from one member to the other" (Sarantakos 1996, p. 14). However, whilst making much of the nature of open systems, particularly in relation to relative 'health'—connections to other systems are seen as the sign of a healthy system—these criteria are referenced against the norms of the nuclear family. There is no context for the family system, there is no environment, either informational or material. There is no sense of the development of this group, of their position in terms of capital and power. Missing from this analytic framework is any indication that families and individuals are constructed within economic and political currents. There *is* a concern with identifying the patterns of stability that characterize effectively functioning, 'healthy' families. These patterns are described in terms of 'feedback' (Sarantakos 1996). As in Structural Functionalism, this is a fundamentally static vision. Issues of individual difference are reduced to subsets of the larger familial system and explained by reference to psychological and universal developmental stages. So, at their core, Systems Theory influenced approaches are premised upon assumptions drawn from psychology—particular models of development and an interest in identifying remediatory agendas. While attempting to understand family as an open system, the use of psychology to identify and categorize individual, or unit, dysfunction inserts a normative and ultimately closed framework—closed in terms of latitude for divergence from 'normal' patterns of development or behaviour.

Noller and Fitzgerald (1993) take the position that "systems theory focuses on the family as a system in which each element affects every other element in predictable and systematic ways" (p. 40). They go on to differentiate between open and closed family systems in terms of health and dysfunction. Closed systems are seen to be dysfunctional families whose closure may mean that members lack the opportunity to compare and realign their own family's practices and values with other 'normal' families[7]. This is an important point—there is a set of approved 'normal' behaviours and practices against which individuals and families should reference themselves. That is, the concept of 'open' at work here refers not to generative, innovative systems but to their compatibility to the aforementioned normative benchmarks. There is an emphasis on predictability and regularity, then, in such systems models, and on normative behavioural guidelines--what amounts to an approved formula for familial health. This established a well-defined and regulated set of boundaries between health and dysfunction. These boundaries are drawn directly from the nuclear family narrative—that specific set of behavioural and relational norms. This narrative has been used as a measure of normalcy and thereby a justification of labels of dysfunction as well as moral decline. While these diagnoses are represented as a therapeutic tool, their connection to larger ideological agendas should not be ignored. Family failure or dysfunction, judged in relation to these specified norms, has given state authorities the opportunity to directly intervene in the functioning of families, even to the extent of removing children and placing them in the care of the State[8]. While I am in no way attempting to downplay the seriousness of these issues and the consequences of family problems, they are however, indicators of nuclear family as a powerful normative and disciplinary agent in Western societies. Further, direct links are made, and acted upon, between individual actions such as truancy or juvenile crime and dysfunctional family. We should continue to ask which groups in our society have the power to attach the label of dysfunction to other groups and individuals. This is particularly true in a time when our own government is making links between its own, quite specific version of family and a strong, stable nation.

The use of Systems Theory in concert with individual psychology was premised upon acceptance of the fundamental nature of the nuclear family to our society at the expense of other family forms. It is against this model of 'normal' familial function that dysfunction is identified and measured. Regardless of whether family therapy or other Systems Theory influenced interventions recognize this, the use of psychology makes it unavoidable. On the basis of these identifications, programmatic interventions are applied to alleviate dysfunction, allowing the family to identify and resume 'normality'. The literature that draws upon this model makes much of

---

[7]   Drawing from cybernetics and general systems theory, the accepted description of closed systems are those systems totally isolated from their environment; open systems are those living systems which are directly responsive to environmental conditions (von Bertalanffy 1968, 1975; Weiner 1954, 1968).

[8]   See also, K. Carrington (1991) for a discussion of the implications of child protection policies within liberal democracies.

familial stability, generally viewed in terms of functional marriage or cohabitation (Becvar & Becvar 1993; Callan & Noller 1987; Gladding 1995; Noller & Fitzpatrick 1993) and measured in relation to examples of normalcy in various aspects of marriage and family, such as sexual activity, familial roles, and parenting. Hence, rather than delivering a new explanatory framing of social life, Systems Theory was coopted by the prevailing politico-economic network, becoming another arbiter of acceptable behaviour within and without the family—a disciplinary mechanism for the Modernist principles of normativity. Systems Theory marked the return of the apolitical and unproblematized nuclear family in light of the challenges of post-war Marxist social theory. It was appealing to many because of its ostensibly neutral scientific language and conceptual framing and its promise of rendering human behaviour transparent and predictable.

Systems Theory has been criticized for over-focussing on the role of the larger system (the family) at the expense of an examination of smaller subsets, for example, parent-child or sibling relationships, and in terms of a deficiency of testable theoretical assertions (Noller & Fitzgerald 1993). In addition, Feminist analyses have argued that Systems Theory and family therapy "helps diminish the personal accountability of family members and their personal responsibility for their actions, encouraging them to blame the family for their personal problems" (Sarantakos 1996, p. 15). I would add that a systems model lacks the theoretical delicacy to deal with issues of changing subjectivity, the movement of individuals through various social fields other than the family system, and the matter of differential kinds and levels of extra-familial capital (Bourdieu 1984; Carrington & Luke 1997). Hence, it can only accommodate a reductionist concept of family. Its major weakness has been its unproblematic acceptance of the nuclear family as a given. This one presumption irrevocably reduces other family forms and relationships to varieties of dysfunction. Thus, despite the initial promise it seemed to offer, Systems Theory failed to reconceptualize views of the family.

CHAPTER 3

THE PRE-1970S POLITICIZED FAMILY

INTRODUCTION

The previous Chapter described and positioned *apolitical* approaches to the family. Unlike apolitical frameworks, politicized approaches are those that view the family, in the first instance, as a site of political and ideological activity. Of significance here are Marxist approaches, and relatedly, The Frankfurt School uptake and critique of the basic tenets of psychology and psychoanalysis. Feminist approaches, in all their theoretical diversity, also understand the family as the site of power relations and political struggle. These critical approaches to the family uncovered the connection between this social form, the social construction of identity, and larger political and economic processes. These approaches do not follow on temporally from apolitical theories of the family—their distinction lies in the way in which they view the role of family and its link to broader social, economic and political processes.

PATRIARCHY AND THE WESTERN NUCLEAR FAMILY—A GIFT FROM GOD

Erich Fromm (1955) tells us that Western culture is founded upon the ancient Jewish and Greek cultures, both of which were patriarchal. According to Fromm the Christian Church played a dominant role in transmitting Jewish and Greek culture, and, along with it, patriarchy, to Europe. The outcome was the rise of rational science and the emergence of the secular state, both enabling conditions for the emergence of the modern nuclear family narrative. The Judeo-Christian tradition generated the moral aspects of patriarchy while its intellectual roots are to be found in Greek culture. In this vein, the predominant European religious ideology, Christianity, clearly chronicles the arrival of humankind in Adam and Eve and their offspring—the first nuclear family. This family, of course, mirrors the patriarchal relationship between God and his people. As Fromm notes (p. 53):

> The crowning and central concept of the patriarchal development of the Old Testament lies, of course, in the concept of God. He represents the unifying principle behind the manifoldness of phenomena.

And, just as the meaning of human existence drew from the existence of God, the nuclear family drew its meaning from the patriarchal male role. Drawing from the model presented by God and recreated in Adam and Eve, the nuclear family has been depicted as the natural human formation, consolidating a belief in the universality and unchanging nature of this family across time and in its hierarchical and patriarchal design. As noted earlier, this coincides nicely with Social Darwinism's notions of the nuclear family as the high point of social evolution. This narrative cum myth has been institutionalized in the dogma of the varieties of Christian Church that have taken Creation as their prime 'truth' and attached to it a normative moral order.

Historical evidence suggests that the Christian Churches, their advocates and employees have long been proactive in ensuring the connection between nuclear family, religious affiliation and the State. As early as the fourth century, Christian religious institutions manoeuvred to replace extended kinship attachments with fealty to the Church itself—God, Church and individual became the pivotal relationship. Rather than loyalty to extended family, the Church required loyalty from each individual unto itself. As part of this shift, marriage and inheritance procedures were formalized in line with Church doctrine, legitimizing and naturalizing a patriarchal nuclear family formation that coincided with economic changes heralding the arrival of capitalism. These new avenues of inheritance acted additionally to diminish the legal and social rights of women and wives, putting them increasingly at the mercy of male family members (Ariés 1962). In this same period, the changes wrought by industrialization and waged employment acted to lessen the pressure for relatives to cooperate in order to work joint pastoral or agricultural holdings and sent increasing numbers to urban centers in search of employment. The increasing dependence upon written records that accompanied this process ultimately benefited the literate male clergy and the institution they represented in terms of social power and in relation to material wealth, particularly the acquisition of land by the Church (Goody 1983, 1996; Haralambos et al. 1996). Indeed, the hand of God had little to do with the Church's eleventh century position as the biggest landholder in France and Britain. Thus, the Church has, for its own purposes, actively sought the maintenance of the nuclear family form, both in terms of social narrative and state legislature. Embedded within this ecclesiastical and State promotion of a particular family form is a prescriptive description of appropriate internal relationships that fed into and reflected the sociocultural and economic environment of the times. Thus, what became an idealized family form was consistently patriarchal in form and function, embodying the persistent ideological commitment to a hierarchical social relationship of sex (gender) role domination and subordination. This, in turn, was tied to particular political agendas, both secular and ecumenical.

Ariés (1962) makes a connection between the need for privacy and space in the shift toward the modern family. He paints a picture of a cramped and public existence as the norm until the end of the seventeenth century—not until the eighteenth century did housing which allowed the development of the modern family become widely available. In its infancy, the modern family was a social form restricted to the nobility and the well-to-do. Ariés suggests that the modern family has remained unchanged from this time to the present, spreading out to other social classes to the point at which "family life finally embraced nearly the whole of society, to such an extent that people have forgotten its aristocratic and middle-class origins" (1962, p.

404). Interestingly, he links the modern family with "intolerance towards variety" and "insistence on uniformity" (p. 415)—this homogeneity is a key and often-unremarked characteristic of the nuclear family. Crucially, 'childhood' as a concept can also be traced to this time. Ariés (1962) argued that the emergence of the concept of the modern family coincides with that of childhood in the sixteenth and seventeenth centuries. What Ariés gives us is a weave of influences—changes in housing, economic change and increasing class differentiation, the emergence of childhood—which came together in the emergence and dissemination of the nuclear family form throughout the various social classes. As we have seen, accompanying and enhancing these changes were the political manipulations of the Church and emergent secular nationstates. And, resting behind these processes was an emerging capitalism, gaining momentum and influence. The nuclear family was rapidly becoming a primary interchange point, holding all these currents together.

MARXIST APPROACHES

Focussing more directly on the impact of industrialization, a Marxist lens on the family made direct links between the reconceptualization of individuals in terms of labor and the emergence of an exploitative social system based around commodity production. Prior to the mid-1800s, family research was characterized by an extended 'preresearch' period featuring non-empirical compilations of family genealogies, household budgets and unemployment assessments by interested amateurs and historians. However, the publication of Engels' *The Origin of the Family, Private Property and the State* (1972) marked a watershed in studies of the family. At this point, interest in family moved from a practical measurement of its characteristics or appeal to a moral order to its position as a social site within an industrializing economy. Engels perceived the family as a highly politicized social organization and his deliberations regarding the family within industrial society precipitated ongoing research interest in the origins of this formation along with the connections between family and the major social institutions.

Of particular importance was his insertion of the value of labor into discussions of human evolution. These theorizations coincided with the spread of Social Darwinism, fed by both evolutionary theory and widespread intellectual interest in notions of social revolution. His interest in the family was at its sharpest when he turned his attention to a consideration of the patriarchal, monogamous family. Drawing upon his own investigations and those he carried out in collaboration with Marx, Engels identified:

> three principal forms of marriage which correspond broadly to the three principal stages of human development: for the period of savagery, group marriage; for barbarism, pairing marriage; for civilisation, monogamy supplemented by adultery and prostitution (1972, p. 138).

It was, however, only for men that monogamy could be supplemented; for women the modern marriage was monogamous, a monogamy enforced by social subordination and legal sanction. Engels, drawing upon the works of Lewis Morgan

(1876, 1963)[9], correlates changes in family form with change in the prevailing mode of production (Haralambos et al. 1996). In this, Engels' representation of linearity parallels that of apolitical perspectives on the family. Influenced by the ancient Greeks, Engels suggests that the "sole exclusive aims of monogamous marriage were to make the man supreme in the family and to propagate, as the future heirs to his wealth, children indisputably his own" (1972, p. 128). Further to this, he summarizes his position regarding the development of monogamy and hence, the nuclear family:

> Monogamy arose from the concentration of considerable wealth in the hands of a single individual—a man—and from the need to bequeath this wealth to the children of that man and no other. For this purpose, the monogamy of the woman was required, not that of the man, so this monogamy of the woman did not in any way interfere with open or concealed polygamy on the part of the man (1972, p. 138).

Engels concludes that modern society rests upon gender-based slavery, arguing that, "the modern individual family is founded on the open or concealed domestic slavery of the wife, and modern society is a mass composed of these individual families as its molecules" (1972, p. 137). The only solution to this form of slavery is to "bring the whole female sex back into public industry, and that this in turn demands that the characteristic of the monogamous family as the economic unit of society be abolished" (1972, p. 138). However, he believed that the evolution of human societies had not reached its conclusion. In line with this view, Engels associated the development of monogamy with the advent of the nuclear family and the requirements of capitalist production. This form of marriage is seen by Engels to involve the subordination of one sex by the other, that is, the dominance of male over female—a dominance linked directly to the economic advantage of men. This is a very different perspective on the nuclear family than that which later characterized Structural Functionalism and Systems Theory. Far from the harmonious, efficiently modern social formation described by apolitical perspectives, this was blatantly exploitative. This family was the bedrock of an exploitative and unsympathetic society. Engels predicted the coming of a social revolution that would end capitalist exploitation, including the subjugation of women. The nuclear family, then, was one aspect of the cycle of capitalist exploitation. Marxist theory argued that the trajectory of progress would inevitably end the capitalism of which the nuclear family was part. Thus, Engels chronicled the increasing regulation of sexual activity (1972) and socially sanctioned production of children (Haralambos 1980) within a patriarchal capitalist system, making a direct link to the system of production and inheritance. Both Marx and Engels understood this inheritance-based division between men and women as the "first division of labor" (1972, p. 129), and Engels went on to discuss the nature of the household in terms of monogamous marriage. Here, he identified the conceptual and social gap instituted between public and private which enables the nuclear narrative:

---

[9]   Based on ethnographic research among the American Indians, Morgan, influenced by the evolutionary theories of Spencer and Darwin, identified human stages of development from "barbarism" to "civilization", which corresponded to particular forms of production.

> With the patriarchal family and still more with the single monogamous family, a change came. Household management lost its public character. It no longer concerned society. It became a private service; the wife became the head servant, excluded from all participation in social production (1972, p. 137).

We can identify a clear conflation of 'family' with the physical and economic site of the 'household'.

Initial Marxist observations of the division between public and private were taken up by Zaretsky (1976) who argued, "that the family in modern capitalist society creates the illusion that the 'private life' of the family is quite separate from the economy". He explicitly linked this separation to the onset of factory production and the requirement for workers to move outside the home in order to take part in this productive cycle (Haralambos et al. 1996). Thus, in Zaretsky's reading, the division between public and private fostered by capitalism became implicated in the illusion of family as a haven rather than a crucial site of commodity consumption and consumer production characterizing apolitical perspectives. Following on from Zaretsky, the private-public division continues to be addressed by Feminist theorists in relation to the lives and experiences of women.

Like Freud and Parsons, neither Marx nor Engels demonstrated an understanding of the conflation of gender and sex identified in recent Feminist writings. Their theories reflect the sociohistorical context in which they worked and consequently, this model was premised upon a productive, waged worker who was identified in class terms above all others and known, beyond doubt, to be male. As another consequence, ethnic and racial diversity played no part in the original Marxist model of capitalist activity—these characteristics were subordinated to class position, that is, to position vis-a-vis the cycle of capitalist production. Identification as proletarian, bourgeois or capitalist, that is, in terms of broad labor categories, became a theoretical and political designation with no conceptual room for sub-category difference.

The Frankfurt School—Marcuse, Adorno, Horkheimer, Fromm

A Marxist perspective on the family was further elaborated in what become known as The Frankfurt School. The intellectual core of this initial group consisted of German Marxists in exile in interwar USA, theorists such as Marcuse, Pollock, Adorno, Horkheimer and Fromm. While not sharing a common view, these theorists were connected by their development of Critical Theory, a multidisciplinary research project that attempts to "construct a systematic, comprehensive social theory that can confront the key social and political problems of the day" (Kellner 1989, p. 1). Underwritten by an emancipatory project, Critical Theory emerged in a time of Modernist economic and social crisis, seeking to understand the new society that was emerging. As Kellner (1989) notes, Critical Theory is positioned as a critique of modernity and the state capitalism associated with it. He sees it as an attempt "to sort out the matrix of progressive and repressive, oppressive and emancipatory, forces bound up with the history of modernity" (1989, p. 4). Part of this project was, according to Jay (1973, p. 116), "a response to the failure of traditional Marxism to explain the reluctance of the proletariat to fulfil its historical role". Where, they asked, was the revolution?

The Frankfurt School delivered a materialist critique, arguing that the ways in which we each view the world and construct theories in order to explain it are historically located. As Horkheimer (cited in Kellner 1989, p. 29) contends, "materialism, unlike idealism, always understands thinking to be the thinking of particular men within a particular period of time. It challenges every claim to autonomy of thought". By its nature, Critical Theory is dialectical and thus follows a trajectory of oppositional understandings, overtaken by syntheses as it deals with the issues of Modernity. This body of work should be viewed as a moment of High Modernism—as a critique of the Modernist construction of the social world from within. Following its Marxist roots, Critical Theory has been concerned with a critical analysis of the social conditions which act to produce ongoing human misery and beyond this, with positioning itself as "an instrument of social transformation which would serve the interests of increasing human freedom, happiness and well-being" (Kellner 1989, p. 32). The family within capitalism becomes, then, a logical site of investigation. This is substantially different from the apolitical view of family as the context in which investigations of individuals and their relationships could take place. Here the family itself and its role in the maintenance of unequal power relations was a focus. In relation to the western family, The Frankfurt School note (1972, p. 130):

> At first sight the family appears in history as a relationship of natural origin, which then differentiates itself to become modern monogamy and which by virtue of this differentiation founds a special domain, the domain of private life. For naive consciousness this private life appears as an island in the state of nature, as it has been idealized. In reality the family not only depends on the historically concrete social reality, but is socially mediated down to its innermost structure.

This is far removed from the view that the nuclear family is a natural outcome of social and economic evolution; that it exists because it represents an essential human social pattern. They go on to describe the changing role of the family within the shift to mass production and the emergence of mass media:

> the family became an agency for society: it trained its members for the assimilation to society; it shaped the human beings in such a manner that they became capable of the tasks which the social system demanded of them (The Frankfurt Institute 1972, p. 136).

Again, The Frankfurt School demonstrates theoretical allegiance to the notion that family cannot be understood in isolation from the society and the social processes in which it is embedded.

The family is thus always an historical site as are the theories used to frame it. Compare this awareness of social construction within political and ideological currents with the apolitical notion of family as a private haven where personality is stabilized and individuals assume preordained social roles. These perspectives understand the positioning and function of the family in fundamentally different ways. This is obvious. However, and this is a key point, these antagonistic approaches share the assumption that the family about which they theorize is the modern nuclear family. Apolitical perspectives construct the nuclear family as the natural family form for modern life; politicized views argue that this family is not natural but is, in fact, constructed within certain political, ideological and economic currents. The politicized family serves particular political and ideological agendas. Both perspectives, however, assume that the family in question is the *nuclear* family.

Fromm, Horkheimer and Marcuse were instrumental in studies which identified the connections between family and authority, marking specifically the ways in which economic factors impact upon family and the relationships between family and authority (Kellner 1989). Fromm argued that a synthesis of Marxist and Freudian theory would "immeasurably enrich materialist social theory...by providing analysis of the mediations through which psyche and society interact and reciprocally shape each other" (Kellner 1989, p. 38). This position was extended by Fromm's suggestion that all societies reproduce authority via the libidinal structures influencing each individual. Fromm's interest in economic processes and the development of identity led him to identify character traits that typified differing phases of capitalism. Capitalism, Fromm's work suggested, created in individuals the characteristics—what Bourdieu (1984; 1992) would call the 'habitus'—most suited to its needs.

Following Fromm's lead, the Frankfurt Institute developed an interest in the relationship between the family—understood as the nuclear bourgeois family—and authority. In Kellner's interpretation, "the studies were concerned with how economic factors influenced the family and how family socialization constituted attitude toward authority" (1989, p. 41). In order to understand this process of social construction, a number of The Frankfurt School theorists turned to psychoanalysis and psychology. The subordination and domination patterns inherent in family authority and broader social structures were highlighted and linked to the production of ego and super ego (Kellner 1989). Unlike the synthesis of psychology and Systems Theory, Critical Theorists were driven to understand the construction of individuals within capitalist society. Marxist theory was not equipped to consider subjectivity, and this was profoundly unsatisfying on some levels. Over time, differing attempts at the creation of a social psychology which synthesized Marxist theory and psychoanalysis were undertaken. These were directed at theorizing the construction of subjectivity in modern capitalism. McCarthy (1976, p. xix) reminds us that:

> it was a characteristic tenet of the early Frankfurt School that basic psychological concepts had to be integrated with basic socioeconomic concepts because the perspectives of an autonomous ego and an emancipated society were essentially interdependent. In this way, critical theory was linked to a concept of the autonomous self that was, on the one hand, inherited from German Idealism but was, on the other hand, detached from idealist presuppositions in the framework of psychoanalysis.

Fromm's interest in psychoanalysis and his project to synthesize Freudian and Marxist theory led him directly to the bourgeois family and an analysis of the allocation of universality given this form of social organization (1970). The bourgeois family was revealed as a primary site of social and class socialization, a position legitimized by the weighting given family in relation to individual development by psychoanalysis.

Shifting emphasis to the impact of the broader society on the function of family, Horkheimer's position was that contemporary capitalism was bypassing the family and other specialist socialization institutions, and tending to directly socialize individuals via the indirect capillaries of mass culture (Arato 1982; Horkheimer 1982; Horkheimer & Adorno 1987; Kellner 1989). In essence, the emergence of a commodified, mass culture was creating a totally manipulated and 'administered' society. Taking this line, the nuclear family becomes a means of administration—a normative narrative. This was exactly the point of Marcuse's (1956, 1964) critical analyses of contemporary capitalist culture and the fate of the individual. Of The Frankfurt School theorists, it was Marcuse who most directly approached a synthesis of Marx and Freud. Marcuse addressed aspects of Freudian theory, in particular, the assertion that "civilization is based on the permanent subjugation of the human instincts" (1956, p. 3). As Habermas notes (1976, p. 71), "the cornerstone of psychoanalysis is the idea that social controls arise from the struggle between instinctual and social needs, from a struggle within the individuals". In relation to the family, he notes, "it is precisely this intrapsychic confrontation that is supposed to have become obsolete in the totally socialized society, which, so to speak, undercuts the family and directly imprints collective ego ideals on the child" (p. 71).

In tune with the transformative and emancipatory agenda of The Frankfurt School, Marcuse searched for an alternative to repression and oppression—his philosophical project to negate the conditions obstructing freedom and happiness (Kellner 1991). He sought an avenue to the "transformation of the libido" which would ultimately reshape the "monogamic and patriarchal family" (Marcuse 1956, p. 201). In effect, Marcuse took Freud's genitally-based notions of libido and sexuality and extended them to the whole person, and beyond, to society. Drawing from Marx, Marcuse understood that the way in which capitalism subjugated the individual was to programme her libido. This analysis mounted a challenge to the patriarchal family revealing it as an instrument of repression and oppression. By this account, this institution, beyond all others, was implicated in the control of libido and the learned acceptance of repressive authority. In *One Dimensional Man* (1964) Marcuse revisited the insight that technology had delivered mass consumption and stifling oppression in the form of the "technological society". As an agent of socialization, the family had been bypassed by other agencies:

> As early as the preschool level, gangs and radio, and television set the pattern for conformity and rebellion; deviations from the pattern are punished not so much within the family as outside and against the family. The experts of mass media transmit the required values; they offer the perfect training in efficiency, toughness, personality, dream, and romance. With this education, the family can no longer compete (1956, p. 97).

Here, Marcuse identified a shift away from the patriarchal family as the central mechanism of control to the forces of mass media. However, what Marcuse also signalled was the increasing pressure on families to conform to a set of normative patterns or principals. While the mass media act upon individuals to construct particular identities and characteristics, this was complemented by the family's increasingly normative role. This shifted the emphasis away from family as a location of personality development to a disciplinary machine in the service of an ideological agenda. Thus, the family identified by these Critical Theorists is vastly different to the one described by Structural Functionalism, Systems Theory or derivatives. The lesson to be learned from Marcuse, in particular, is that sociological representations of a traditional family cannot be separated from the constructions of the public culture.

However, the shift to postmodernism and late capitalism has seemingly been difficult for Critical Theorists. Kellner's description of this difficulty is worth noting at length:

> if it is the case that new socio-historical conditions, forms and experiences have emerged, then Critical Theory today should obviously analyze, critique and conceptualize these phenomena, and should develop and rethink radical social theory and politics in light of these changes. Most Critical Theorists have not really confronted these challenges, however, and have either attacked postmodernist writing *en masse* from traditional Critical Theory positions (mostly Adorno's) or, like Habermas, have presented ideology critiques of the theories of postmodernism while defending modernity (1989, p. 73).

Thus, while Critical Theory has undoubtedly much to offer analyses of new times and the sociopolitical outcomes of globalization, it has not yet travelled this theoretical pathway. It seems evident, then, that Critical Theory tends to be linked more closely with nationstate capitalism and has not, as yet, adequately theorized the emergence of a new stage in the history of capitalism and the nationstate. It remains focussed on the nuclear family as its unit of analysis.

The work of The Frankfurt School (1972) stands in clear counterpoint to interactionism and Structural Functionalism. This is a recognition of the strong position of apolitical approaches to the family in the post World War Two years. Returning for a moment to the historical context in which these approaches developed it is easy to understand the western world's ideological investment in the nuclear family. However, rather than adopting the somewhat contradictory Functionalist position that the family, although the basic building block of society, somehow existed outside that society's political processes, the theorists of The Frankfurt School perceived the family to be enmeshed in broader social contexts and in time. They argued that the fate of the family was dependent on the larger social process rather than as a "self-sufficient social form" (1972, p. 144). That is, the family cannot *but* be socially mediated in all aspects and becomes, in this reading, implicated in socializing individual members into an acceptance of and role within, the exploitations of capitalist production.

FEMINIST THEORY AND THE FAMILY

The theorists of The Frankfurt School also demonstrated an interest in the social status and roles of women although this was limited by pre-established notions of gender roles. Adorno, in particular, held the belief that women may hold the key to defeating fascism (Jureidini et al. 1997), however this hope for a woman-led resistance to this process of totalitarianism was based upon the traditional female role of responsibility for human relationships, reinforcing the image of women's containment in the private sphere. However, whilst Critical Theory generalized sex and gender and social roles, the theorists of The Frankfurt School recognized the exploitation of unpaid and unacknowledged female labour within the private domain of the family. This domestic labour exists outside recognized capitalist modes of production, bolstered by, and upholding, the socially subordinate positioning of women within an ostensibly democratic and equitable social system. Whilst women were understood to be no more resistant to totalitarian manipulation than any other social group regardless of their presumed nurturing nature, Frankfurt School theorists did foreground a contradiction in the democratic ideal of equality (Jureidini et al. 1997) that has been seized upon by Feminist theorists.

During the 1960s and 1970s, feminist writers began to make use of Marxist perspectives to analyse the family in capitalism and the position of women within it (Benston 1972; Firestone 1970; Hartmann 1979; Mitchell 1971). Osmond and Thorne suggest that:

> Feminists have been drawn to Marxist theories because they stress not only power relations, but also the point of view of the oppressed....(and) have drawn upon these insights while revising Marxist traditions to make women's subordination and gender relations more central (1993, p. 595).

These Marxist analyses focussed on the wife as societal 'safety-valve' in her role as emotional support for an economically productive husband, the uncalculated costs of household labour (Dalla Costa & James 1975; Delphy 1984; Ironmonger 1989), and the role of the family in conditioning acceptance of capitalist class position (Feeley 1972). This direction was extended by Oakley's (1974, 1976, 1982) and Firestone's (1970) analyses problematizing the connection of women with motherhood. Prior to this, a number of non-Marxist and pre-feminist analyses of the family emerged in the late nineteenth and early twentieth century. Gillman's *Women and Economics* (1966) argued that the economic power of the male within the family made waged work for women essential for self-esteem, while Margaret Mead's pre-feminist critiques of the family led her to argue, in the early 1900s, that less restrictive attitudes to sex and motherhood would result in less familial conflict (Osmond & Thorne 1993). These initial analyses focussed on the labor carried out by women—childbirth, housework, childrearing—however their major long-term contribution was to problematize essentialist notions of womanhood and family. Even these early critiques identified the high cost paid by women for the illusion of harmonious families and a stable society.

As a mode of analysis, feminist theory resists affiliation with any specific disciplinary strand, cutting across boundaries in its emphasis on relations of power and lens on the opacity of ideology. Without seeking to generalize across the complex multiplicity of feminist agendas and positions, this approach takes as its constitutive premise the exploitation and oppression of women and other marginalized groups in a male-dominated society. According to Tong (1989, p. 1), who characterizes feminist thought as a kaleidoscope:

> feminist theory is not one, but many, theories or perspectives and each feminist theory or perspective attempts to describe women's oppression, to explain its causes and consequences, and to prescribe strategies for women's liberation. The more skilfully a feminist theory can combine description, explanation, and prescription, the better that theory is.

However, in general, feminist theories can be placed under the umbrella headings of liberal, Marxist, radical, psychoanalytic, socialist, or postmodern (Tong, 1989). For liberal feminists, the achievement of gender equality—a level playing field—in the public sphere is paramount, while for Marxist feminists equality is impossible given the structural inequalities which result from capitalism and its system of private ownership. The term 'radical feminism' refers to a diverse range of positions focussing on the connections of sex and femininity, and the ways in which these have been used to subjugate women. Thus, constructions of sexuality are a core interest for radical feminists, particularly in their connection to the oppression of women. Linking the diverse and evolving strands of radical feminism is a belief that patriarchy is at the source of gender constructions (Tong 1989) and, that these constructions act to the disadvantage of women.

Approaching the subordination of women within patriarchal society from a differing perspective, psychoanalytic feminism has taken as its starting point the psychosocial theories of Freud, in many instances attempting to reconstruct the Freudian notion of femaleness as lack (Chodorow 1989, 1994; Dinnerstein 1977; Mitchell 1974; Ortner 1975) or, existentially, 'otherness' (de Beauvoir 1974). This has led to their separation of the issue of gender difference from that of male domination (Young 1984), and their work towards the development of a model which foregrounds the role of women in the development of children (Irigaray 1991; Klein 1975a, 1975b). However, reconstructions and reconfigurations of Oedipus, feminist or otherwise, ultimately validate its legitimacy and the gender codes it represents (Sprengnether 1995). Rather than reconfiguring Oedipus to more fairly represent females, Sprengnether argues that Oedipus itself should be questioned. Linked to this argument, Sprengnether offers an astute and concise description of the genesis and significance of the Oedipus complex. Keen to understand Freud contextually, she writes:

> An outgrowth of Freud's intense introspection following his father's death in 1896, the Oedipal construct acquired its status as the 'nuclear complex'....(when) Freud first referred to the 'Oedipus Complex' in his 1910 essay, 'A special type of choice made by men', where he connects it to the boy's anguish at discovering his mother's sexual activity (and hence unfaithfulness) with his father. Once he had settled on this term, Freud tied it to a more ambitious project, that of explaining the evolution of human

civilization. In *Totem and Taboo* (1913)...Freud locates the Oedipus complex at the very
origin of human culture (p. 159).

For Freud, then, the Oedipus complex was both ontogenetic and phylogenetic. Freud
tied oedipal repression inextricably to the processes of human civilization and to the
normal development of the individual. In a key move, these presumptions were
unproblematically tied to a hierarchical gender order and a specific cultural frame.
Thus, Oedipus, in its unswerving emphasis on the role of the father in the
development of sexuality, and ultimately the healthy individual, feeds directly to and
directly from a patriarchal social order. Again, Sprengnether—herself a
psychoanalytic feminist—is useful in pinpointing the impact of Oedipus, noting that
it "decides one's sexual and cultural identity with a single phallic stroke" (1995, p.
159). It is this emphasis on the normative agenda of Oedipus that Deleuze and
Guattari build upon and extend in their radical philosophy (see Chapter 4).

Reflecting the deep-seated acceptance of the oedipalized relations, which
characterize 'normal' nuclear families, not until the voices of black feminists began
to gain volume and gather momentum, was there a concerted challenge to the
normalcy of the homogeneously white, male-headed nuclear family. Black feminist
writers, in particular, have challenged the normative idealization of nuclear family
(Collins 1991; hooks 1981, 1989, 1992). In its stead, they highlight the strength and
value of one parent families, of intergenerational and extended family links, and of
fictive kinship ties. In particular, black feminist thought has highlighted the
importance and validity of female-headed families, arguing that white and male
notions of motherhood need to be reconceptualized (Christian 1985; Collins 1991;
Joseph 1984, Osmond & Thorne 1993). However, until the principles of
normativity—the acts of institutional symbolic violence which construct particular
identities within capitalist societies are identified and reformed, these demands for
recognition will remain subordinate to, and measured against, the mainstream
narrative of the nuclear family.

Adopting a more eclectic approach, socialist feminism has acted to synthesize, or
weave together, many of the themes of other feminist theories in order to more
adequately frame the experiences of women. In this sense, it attempts to create an
integrated feminist theory (Tong 1989), and consequently, the specific interests of
socialist feminist theorists overlap with those of other feminist theorists in various
areas. Postmodern feminists, however, are not interested in unified theory.
Reflecting the recent emergence of postmodernism, theirs is not an agenda of
unification but rather a concern to recognize the multiplicity and complexity of
feminist theories. Accompanying this is a rejection of the possibility of any one
'true' feminist theory or narrative.

Notwithstanding their vast diversity, these differing outlooks are underpinned by an
interest in identifying, explaining, and attempting to redress, women's oppression.
Foregrounded here is the construction of subjectivity by the broader economic,
language and social system. In this perspective, "it is not that the subject speaks, but

rather the subject is spoken through by discourse, law, culture" (Grosz 1990, p. 68). Thus, the nuclear family narrative and the notion of 'woman' that accompanied it are not to be taken as natural or neutral. Instead, they are to be understood as outcomes or symptoms of larger, politicized processes. Thus, feminist analysis of the family forms one aspect of a larger philosophical project. Barrett and McIntosh (1991) report that, together, the many feminist theories have "drawn attention to the violence and degradation hidden within the walls of the nuclear household, and to the broader social and economic inequalities connected with it" (p. 19). Associated with this problematization is a "concern with the sexual objectification of woman and the exploitation of wives and mothers" (p. 19). These approaches give an instructive insight into the ways in which the exploitation and subjugation of women made possible the ideological constructions of identity, nation, community and family characteristic of nationstate capitalism.

In relation to the family as a site of feminist analysis, Osmond and Thorne (1993, p. 618) observe that:

> Much of traditional family sociology starts by assuming that women are inseparable from the family; this is quite different from Feminists' insistence on placing women's own experiences at the centre of analysis and recognizing gender as a basic structural feature, not only of families, but of all other institutions.

Thus, in their emphasis on women, feminist analyses have disregarded the closed systems approach where an ideological boundary between the home and society masks the complex positioning of individuals and family in social life. Feminist theory has aggressively challenged the ideological division between the private home and a public economic sphere enshrined in traditional, ahistorical approaches to the family. Overall, the feminist agenda has, at various times, focused particularly on the constructions of gender, race, class and ethnicity (Gunew 1994; Gunew & Yeatman 1993) which act to empower some social groups at the expense of others. It is tuned particularly to the experiences of women within landscapes of social power. Thus, for many feminist approaches, the family is the institutional locus of patriarchal exploitation—not only of women, but also the aged, the non-white', the young, and even men. In response, the primacy of patriarchy is problematized by accounts which foreground the role of women in western culture (see, for example, Irigaray 1991). The interdisciplinary nature of feminist theory allows critiques of power and gender relations that move beyond the family unit into the macro level of social structures and activity. Rather than understanding the family as a closed, private site, these analyses position it within politicized social relationships. For feminists, the family is one site of these relations—a site ideologically linked to the sanctioned role and identity of womanhood in our society. The family, as the designated 'private' site with which women have been ideologically and economically associated became one site of feminist analysis. This 'family' has in turn been understood in terms of the nuclear family narrative, with its implicit normative parameters. Even those branches of feminist theory which reject the nuclear canon, such as the work of lesbian, black and some radical feminists, recognize the normative role this formation has played within contemporary Western society and construct their agendas in response.

Conclusion

Apolitical approaches to the family constructed and maintained a particular narrative of the modern family and of Western culture, preferring to view it as an uncontested social space. These approaches took the nuclear family form as a given, thereby accepting particular assumptions about the roles and relationships which form this social dynamic and between 'the family' and other social and economic fields. Inbuilt presumptions about internal familial relationships draw upon Freudian notions of sexuality and desire, requiring that the nuclear family construct itself in relation to these culturally and historically specific regulatory expectations. Against the backdrop of American technological and cultural hegemony and the reality of a booming capitalist cycle within separate nations, theorizations of family obfuscate the specific cultural and historical conditions which made possible the modern nuclear family. For some time Critical Theory stood alone in suspecting the naturalness of the family and of the principles of normativity which operated through it. However, as in apolitical framings, this family was unproblematically taken to be nuclear. This one particular family formation became a *nuclear narrative* that outlined how to live and just as importantly, how not to live.

CHAPTER 4

CRITIQUES FROM WITHIN: POST-1970S MODERNIST CRITIQUES AND THE NUCLEAR NARRATIVE

INTRODUCTION

In the late 1960s and early 1970s[10], a series of events including worldwide student riots, the emergence of organized terrorism, the OPEC oil crises and the assassinations of American leaders shook the foundations of Modernity. Out of this destabilization a new generation of social critiques emerged which extended the work of earlier politicized accounts. There was a shift in emphasis—where earlier approaches were concerned (or not) with the family as a site of capitalism exploitation and source of human unhappiness, these later theories were particularly interested in how it is that we are made to do and to be. In all these approaches there is an explicit concern with identifying and critiquing the principles of normativity these theorists believed underwrote the existing phase of capitalism. This Chapter brings together and reinterprets a number of these analytic projects: the radical philosophical project of Deleuze and Guattari (1983, 1987), the politicized and fluid social-material integration of Pierre Bourdieu's sociological method (1973, 1977a, 1977b, 1977c, 1984, 1990, 1991, 1994); and the ecosystemic logic of Anthony Wilden's Context Theory (1975, 1978a, 1978b, 1981, 1980, 1987).

AN ECOSYSTEMIC ANALYSIS OF THE NUCLEAR FAMILY

Before turning to the highly specific critiques of Oedipus and symbolic violence characteristic of the work of Deleuze and Guattari, and Bourdieu, it would be · strategic to pull back to a broader framing of the capitalist system and the role of the family within it. We therefore begin this chapter with Wilden's ecosystemic framing of capitalism. Like the work of Bourdieu and that of Deleuze and Guattari, this framing attempted to highlight the politicized nature of social life and the role of ideology in its reproduction. To make this analysis of capitalism, Anthony Wilden developed a wide-ranging theoretical framework. The sources of what he termed

---

[10] In 1968, often marked as a watershed in modern history, Robert Kennedy and Martin Luther King were assassinated in the USA; civil unrest broke out across the Western world; the Vatican released the encyclical *Humanae Vitae* rejecting artificial contraception while Britain legalized abortion on demand; Saddam Hussein led the coup which installed him in power in Iraq; in Indonesia, Suharto was ousted from power by Sukarno; the Baader-Meinhof terrorist organization was formed; French students and workers rioted in Paris; Brezhnev sent Soviet tanks into Czechoslovakia; and, Harold Holt disappeared in the Australian surf.

"Context Theory"[11] were wide-ranging, drawn from critical analyses of Lévi-Srauss and Piaget, communication theory and the theory of double bind, from semiotics and from Marx's sense of the fundamental role of the economic system in determining the nature of human relationships. Wilden sought a theoretical framing with the potential to critically evaluate existing patterns of domination and subordination, which in Wilden's estimation, were ultimately sourced in the prevailing economic deep-structure of capitalism. This framework must, in addition, position these patterns within larger contexts of matter-energy and sociocultural (informational) systems. Wilden noted that:

> although the organic and human worlds are ultimately subject to the laws of the physical universe, they also obey laws that have no application in physics or chemistry. For whereas the classical physical universe is a universe primarily of matter-energy, the organic and human universe is one primarily of information (1975, p. 93).

To accomplish this task, he turned to the notion of logical levels—organizational hierarchies of dependence. To put it simply, Wilden argued that no one system could exist outside the influence of others—each system exists in relation to a context. Wilden believed that a framework based upon 'real' hierarchies of dependence would be less inclined to insulate human sociocultural and economic systems from an understanding of their ultimate dependence upon other systems. Here is a first hint of the usefulness of Wilden's framework for theorizing family—the recognition that all systems are ultimately linked to others. This was Wilden's fundamental indictment of capitalism: as an ideological system it obscures the real relationships of dependency which exist between systems and which lie at the core of capitalist exploitation. That is, capitalist ideology acts to flatten out hierarchical relationships and distort 'reality'. In this framing, the focal construction of the nuclear family contributes to this distortion.

Wilden's ecosystemic understanding is premised upon a view of complex systems— capitalism, families and the individual—as open, dynamic and goal-seeking, but always contextualized. In particular, Wilden focussed on open complex systems as informational, where information is transmitted across and through systems of differing organizational type. Here, information processes (incoming, outgoing, transformations) are directly linked to the goal-seeking activities of open systems. In this account, human societies code and use information to "organize and direct the energy necessary for 'work' to be done by, within or outside the system" (Wilden & Wilson 1976, p. 233). The codings established and maintained within the phase of capitalism with which Wilden was familiar constructed ideologically constrained realities and organized particular 'work'. Prime amongst these realities was the nuclear family. In this view, the nuclear family acted as a device for coding information so that certain constructions of reality were maintained and particular work was carried out. Again, this selective tradition is linked to issues of social

---

[11]   For Wilden (1987, p. 310), Context Theory constituted "a theory oriented to information, goal-seeking, constraint, relationships, reciprocity, levels of reality, levels of responsibility, levels of communication and control, requisite diversity, innovation, openness, cooperation, the capacity to utilize unexpected novelty, and thus towards long-range survival and the future".

power and knowledge. Only some groups' selective traditions become enshrined in the nuclear narrative and this is at the expense of others'.

Capitalism and paradox

Taking the position that scientific and social discourses are "constrained by socioeconomic reality" (1980, p. xxiii), Wilden was consistently critical of capitalism and of the prospects for its long-term survival (Wilden & Wilson 1976; Wilden 1978a, 1978b, 1980). In order to understand the dynamic underwriting the self-destructive and seemingly inexorable progress of capitalism, Wilden drew from the communications work of Bateson (1972, 1979)[12]. By incorporating Bateson's notion of the double bind into his ecosystemic framing, Wilden was able to articulate the paradoxical nature of capitalism:

> the contradictions inherent in the continued growth of capital for the sake of capital...are truly paradoxical. Logically, this means that capitalism views itself as a closed energy system operating in an infinite environment...whereas in fact it is an open system in a finite environment (1978a, p. 88).

Capitalism's paradox, then, becomes the choice between continued expansion towards destruction of the environment and itself, or, an end to expansion and an ensuing spiral to self-destruction. By Wilden's account, the nature of paradox explains the dynamics of open systems, including human systems both organic and social. Taking this concept and applying it to the family, it is possible to make a case that the family can also be explained by paradox—in the case of the family this paradox would be made visible by the generalization of oedipus relationships and the particular shapings of desire and identity that take place within it.

For Wilden, capitalism is linked to the development of particular Western epistemologies centred on an ideological construction of "free and equal and autonomous individuals in open and symmetrical competition in a free marketplace of commodities and ideas" (1978a, p. 74). Thus, in the free marketplace each individual supposedly succeeds or fails on the basis of individual merit. The same would hold true for family forms. This belief is based upon the ideological, as opposed to 'real', collapse of hierarchical positions allowing individuals of unequal social position and power to be discursively represented as equal. Wilden argued that the Western belief in the linear causality of classical physicals underpins this ideological closure. From an ecosystemic perspective it is not possible to talk about linear cause and effect relationships, nor is it possible to 'inadvertently' confuse

---

[12] Gregory Bateson's (1972, 1979) reconceptualization of ecological relationships in terms of information rather than matter-energy and his development of the concept of the double bind were crucial to the development of Wilden's particular ecosystemic perspective. Bateson, along with Watzlawick et al. (1967) are the source of Wilden's view that information controls the dispersal of matter-energy within any system, leading to Wilden's (Wilden & Wilson 1976, Wilden 1980) emphasis on aspects of communication theory and his concern to differentiate between matter-energy and information. The key difference in terms of Wilden's project lies in the recognition that while energy-matter cannot be destroyed, only transformed, information can be both created and destroyed (Wilden & Wilson 1976, Wilden 1980).

organizational, or logical level. Instead, an ecosystemic epistemology requires the understanding that all "processes are interlinked" (Wilden 1978a, p. 74) and occurs across and through systems of differing organizational type. This is the transdisciplinary vocabulary of Wilden's context theory—a vocabulary that attempts to incorporate an understanding of the differential positioning of individuals within social hierarchies of power and within organic and inorganic contexts.

WILDEN'S FAMILY

While his analyses were directed specifically at capitalism as an ideological system, Wilden's central contribution to the study of families was to shatter forever the illusion of closure and autonomy with which this formation was shrouded in apolitical frameworks. He is, however, constrained by the particular theoretical lineage of his own theories. For Wilden, family features as the marker of the boundary between nature and culture, where culture is a temporally frozen, preserved structural characteristic[13] of human society. It is here, in the family, that an exchange system based upon incest prohibition is operationalized. Here, it becomes clear that Wilden's understanding and use of the notion of culture is entirely anthropological and structural.

Wilden's neglect of culture, or rather his purely anthropological use of the concept, has consequences. Without a sociological analysis of culture, this framing of the human world cannot address the changing practices and beliefs that accompany the shifts in capitalism. He is limited to a structuralist reification of social formation. Wilden's hierarchical modelling of real relations between systems is directed toward shaking our faith in the ahistorical nature of capitalism. This it does. It was never his intent to delve into the construction of subjectivities or the changing cultural landscape that exists within these relationships—historically this was a theoretical project that did not emerge until much later.

For Wilden, the Western conceptualization of a nuclear family is a prime exemplar of the atomistic epistemology that prompted his ecosystem approach: the nuclear family "is a notion dependent on an atomistic epistemology which assumes what is to be proved" (1980, p. 246n). That is, there is an assumption that the larger system is composed of an aggregate of smaller units, constituting a linear dependency. This view does not recognize the multiplicity of relationships between society and family units and between each of these units and other systems. Also, and importantly, it "denies the relations within the supersystem of the society which actually generate the family" (1980, p. 246n). Here, Wilden is making the point that it is the larger system that determines the existence of family rather than the nuclear relationship forming the building block of the society as depicted within Functionalism. In an

---

[13]   Wilden chose to draw upon the structuralist anthropology of Lévi-Strauss (1969a, 1969b, 1973) in order to understand the self-imposed boundaries of the nuclear family within capitalism, although this took the form of a brief footnote. See Wilden 1980, p. 246n.

ecosystemic framing, the nuclear family is a moment in a complex set of dynamic interconnections.

Ultimately, Wilden brings into question representations of the nuclear family as the separable and ahistorical building block of advanced society. His descriptions of an ecosystemic reality are far more complex. Where a more simplistic view presents society as an aggregate of these smaller segments, an ecosystemic view understands that the supersystem exists both outside and through this relationship. At the broader level, Wilden has argued the internal paradox of capitalism. In order to understand the punctuation or framing in which human subjects live their lives, the ways in which reality is constructed and perceived, Wilden attempted to critique the socioeconomic relations which he argued underwrite all social relationships. This was both the brilliance and the limitation of Wilden's work. Although he developed an ecosystemic framework breathtaking in its scope and ambition, he could never fully conceptualize the role of cultural formations in macro- and micro-social systems. His analyses of human relationships were drawn directly from double bind theory and from Lacanian reinterpretations of Freud, thus his understanding and use of culture was entirely structuralist. His critique of capitalism was tied to the rise of Rational Man and positivist science, an account that does not incorporate cultural, racial or ethnic difference. Wilden thus remained positioned, however unwillingly, in Modernist understandings of the individual and culture. Thus, although laying the groundwork, he was never able to adequately connect human sociocultural life to ecosystemic processes other than as alienated commodities in an exploitative economic system. For Wilden, following Marx, the only avenue to social change became the shift to an entirely new system, or destruction, and consequently he was attempting to construct a metalanguage which would transcend this double bind. His critique of capitalism remains, however, deeply disturbing. Within this critique, the nuclear family is revealed as a politicized narrative, a set of normative principles which serve ideological purposes. The ways in which these principles operate within the social world becoming, in fact, embodied, can be explained by reference to the sociological theory of Pierre Bourdieu (1977c, 1984, 1990, 1991)[14].

HABITUS AND SYMBOLIC VIOLENCE

Bourdieu's framework centres on the concept of an *economy of practice* wherein all human activity is implicated in the action of social power and different sets of practice have differing valuations across social fields. Thus, all practice is inherently directed at the maximization of social advantage and power. These social relationships take place within a multidimensional space, composed of *fields*: semi-autonomous, structured social spaces characterized by discourse and social activity (Bourdieu 1991; Bourdieu & Wacquant 1992). Each social field is constructed and reconstructed in relation to its own evolution through time and space and to the individuals who operate within it. Individuals and institutions are arranged within

---

[14]   See also Bourdieu & Wacquant 1992; Carrington & Luke 1997.

fields according to relative accumulations of capital, each attempting to maximize and strategically wield their holdings of power and control within each social field.

Each family constitutes, then, a field—a semi-autonomous social space that both creates and is created by individuals. To accept this representation of family as a social field is to abandon, as a consequence, any notion of the nuclear family as the standardized building block of a stable society.

Habitus

The social conditions that determine the discourses and practical activities characteristic of particular fields act in concert with the processes of socialization to develop, in each individual, systems of *habitus*. Bourdieu describes this concept in the oft-cited passage as:

> systems of durable, transposable dispositions, structured structures predisposed to function as structuring structures, that is, as principles of the generation and structuring of practices and representations which can be objectively 'regulated' and 'regular' without in any way being the product of obedience to rules, objectively adapted to their goals without presupposing a conscious aiming at ends or an express mastery of the operations necessary to attain them and, being all this, collectively orchestrated without being the product of the orchestrating action of a conductor (Bourdieu 1977c, p. 72).

For Bourdieu, habitus bridges the social and biological via the construction of flexible, yet structured and embodied dispositions. The inculcation of sociocultural value systems and practices goes beyond the traditional sociological notion of socialization, becoming entrenched in the physical characteristics of individuals. Habitus structures become embodied and hence especially durable. Individuals, then, *embody* the value systems and practical knowledges of the particular fields in which they exist. Habitus is consequently a particularly useful and constitutive way to look at the effect of spatiality on human relationships, bodily hexis and practice— Bourdieu's original usage of the term was directed at understanding the renewal of social hierarchies across generations and in the face of ongoing challenge.

Reference to the habitus is useful for developing a vision of the totality of oedipal symbolic violence—through habitus we can conceptualize the embodiment and naturalization of the normative principles key to oedipus. Family, as a key social field, has a particularly significant impact on the formation of habitus and as a result, the ways in which individuals move through other social spaces. Each individual's position within these various social spaces is dependent, Bourdieu argues, on their differential access to various types of *capital*.

As I have noted elsewhere (Carrington & Luke 1997; Carrington, Mills & Roulston 2000), *capital* has been the most utilized of Bourdieu's sociological concepts. In developing his market framework, Bourdieu conceived four differing capital types (economic, social, cultural and symbolic), each contributing to the positioning of individuals and institutions within various social fields. An academic, for example, has an accumulation of particular types of cultural capital—journal articles, international reputation; economic capital—research funding; and social capital—personal networks of other academics—which establishes his/her value relative to other academics. In this account, the social world operates around ongoing interactions and exchanges between individuals with differing amounts of the various capitals, each encounter taken as an opportunity to either hold or increase social power within particular fields. Arguably, the most crucial of Bourdieu's concepts, the one which underpins his overall sociological framework, is *symbolic violence*.

Symbolic violence

The notion of *symbolic violence* refers to the imposition of cultural systems via habitus formation without connecting these practices to "the power relations which are at their source" (Bourdieu & Passeron 1990, p. 41). This concept is particularly powerful because Bourdieu has linked it quite specifically to the development of bodily hexis. In this, it goes beyond less complex notions of socialization and has the ability to link the individual human into a web of corporeal inculcations, recognizing that practice, or praxis, is simultaneously a physical and social activity. Further, this activity can never be neutral. Corporeity, in this view, is not immune from the symbolic violence that constructs the various realities in which we live.

Throughout Bourdieu's framing the relationship between social life and the physical body remains prime. Physical practices become inscribed into habitus, impacting upon subjectivity and future action. That is, processes of symbolic violence become embodied. The family, as a mechanism of symbolic violence, becomes one of the key sites of habitus formation. Bourdieu has quite explicitly outlined symbolic violence and its relation to the status quo:

> Symbolic violence, to put it as tersely and simply as possible, is the violence which is exercised upon a social agent with his or her complicity....Of all forms of "hidden persuasion", the most implacable is the one exerted, quite simply, by the order of things (Bourdieu & Wacquant 1992, p. 172).

We are all complicit, as Wilden (1980) notes, in our own capture by the dominant normative principles of our society. Always, Bourdieu hinges the action and effectiveness of symbolic violence on the complicit misrecognition of those 'knowing social agents' on whom it is effected. This symbolic violence seems to enter and impact upon us via the very air we breathe and the spaces we inhabit. It is particularly potent because reality always appears self-evident. Further emphasizing the everyday nature of the action of symbolic violence, Bourdieu notes:

> ...the modalities of practices, the ways of looking, sitting, standing, keeping silent, or even of speaking...are full of injunctions that are powerful and hard to resist precisely because they are silent and insidious, insistent and insinuating...(1991, p. 51).

Consider if you will, the nuclear family home—the natural habitat of the nuclear family. Many of us grew up in one and we are aware of the characteristic portioning of space. As Aries (1962) pointed out, particular arrangements of space are linked to the development of the nuclear family in the eighteenth century. As such, the family home provides an interesting 'everyday' illustration of the scope and power of symbolic violence. In the same way that the nuclear family has been depicted as an ahistorical and natural form, the nuclear home has been ideologically constructed as a private haven. More than a physical enclosure, architecture forms one of the central symbolic systems of our society: values, political currents, aspirations and ideologies are enshrined in architectural form, constituting a coded visual communication, a semaphore. Making matters all the more complex is the dual role of architecture—not only is it a communication about the society in which it stands, but it also acts upon those within. It is both formed by and forms culturally immersed individuals within its social and material spaces. This is an intricate relationship of coercion, complicity and resistance—symbolic violence at work.

Bourdieu has been particularly interested in understanding the ways in which knowing social agents become who they are, the processes via which each of us takes on particular value systems and ways of being in the social world. Architecture and the spaces we inhabit are part of this process. The clearly delineated public and private spaces of western domestic housing; the smaller children's rooms; the communal areas; the movement from inside to outside; the positioning and construction of bathroom/toilets and kitchens—these all send unspoken cultural messages about the kinds of people we are to be.

The nuclear family house is interesting in another respect. In our society, the family home has become a consumer product, even an object of desire. In order to purchase and live in our dream home, we are forced to sell our labour and additionally, to sell our *future* labour by taking on considerable debt. If one were cynical it would be very easy to make a link between the myth of nuclear family, the nuclear dream home and the consumption-debt cycle underpinning globalizing capitalism. Family home becomes another way of buying an identity in our consumer society—our purchase conveys our commitment to fitting in, to being good worker-citizens. In effect, we send a signal to those around us when we purchase a family home. This is all fascinating and saturated with issues around ideology, consumption and identity. However, as we have seen, rather than a site for social analysis, family and family home have become, in Foucault's words, sanctified and thus ideologically removed from real life[15].

This is one of the strengths of Bourdieu's project. His central point is that reality is always a construction that reflects existing distributions of social power, and further, that the reproduction of particular realities serves specific political purposes.

---

[15]   This is particularly interesting given the mass production of housing for the nuclear family which, along with building and marketing defensive capabilities, has fuelled Western economies since the end of post-Second World War hostilities—a superficial glance reveals the connection between economic growth and the spread of mass produced single family dwellings. While the suburban zone has existed for as long as there have been urban centers (see, for example, Mattingly 1997), the massive suburban explosion which has characterized many modern nations, including American and Australia, can be traced to the intricate linkages between economic growth, developments in the technologies of mass production and population growth.

Following this logic, the narrative of the nuclear family is a construction that serves particular ideological visions and political agendas. It can be no other way. For, as natural as the family appears, it is actually the process of symbolic violence that created our particular view that is natural.

Bourdieu thus gives us a framing of the social universe wherein innumerable social fields are constructed in relation to patterns of social power. In each field individuals manoeuvre for advantage using their particular combinations and volumes of the various forms of capital. Our desire for particular types and volumes of capital are embodied in us via symbolic violence. In our society, these processes occur in many ways and sites: the architecture of our homes, popular media representations, folk theories of the good life, analytic models and medical and political discourses. While this is a powerful contribution what makes Bourdieu's work stand out is the inextricable linking of the body with the social. In combination with Wilden's revealing critique of the complicity of ideologies in misunderstandings of interdependencies between and within systems, this is a powerful analysis. Wilden tells us that the naturalness of these power relationships is itself constructed and politicized. Within this framing of the processes of symbolic violence we can now position the channelling of identity and desire that must take place within the family in order for it to fulfil its role in a capitalist system and which can be accessed via reference to the notion of oedipus.

OEDIPUS AND COLONIZATION

The nuclear narrative acts to shape each of us in particular ways which are then taken to be innate characteristics. This shaping is reinforced by a series of social sanctions that apply to those who are considered to have moved outside the boundaries these principles—economic disadvantage, social exclusion, marginalization and even institutionalization. This is a central observation. The point is that oedipus, qua a process of symbolic violence, has become the key principle of normativity in modern society, becoming a measurement against which norms can be reproduced and monitored, and deviance can be identified and judged. I am deviating from the general capitalization of the term 'oedipus' in order to indicate its use in a generalized sense. Here I draw upon the understanding and use of oedipus and capitalism developed by the philosopher Deleuze and activist psychoanalyst Guattari in *Anti-Oedipus: Capitalism and Schizophrenia* (1983). Like Marxist theory their materialist critique understands Modernity and nationstate capitalism as an historical phase. Their particular project is to reconstitute desire as a productive force or machine, challenging notions of an integrated and unitary subject which characterize Modernity. Capitalism becomes a 'flow' whose ability to manifest briefly in physical sites is described as de and re-territorialization. They identify psychoanalysis and the nuclear family as complicit in the repression and moulding of what should be a creative aspect of desire. Oedipus is the process of shaping desire. Best and Kellner (1991, p. 87) observe that:

the thrust of their attack on psychoanalysis is that it transforms machinic desire into a passive theatre of representation that confines desire within the circumscribed field of Oedipus and the family.

Deleuze and Guattari's refusal of oedipus opens a pathway which can avoid binarist representations of reality. Instead, Deleuze and Guattari theorize a fluid and mediated multiple subjectivity. Theirs is a poststructuralist critique of Modernity which is not unrelated to that of Foucault. However, where Foucault focussed on the patterning of knowledge that characterizes various historical moments, Deleuze and Guattari address themselves to the shaping of libidinal flows within capitalist society. They insist upon the fluidity and centrality of desire and its direct connection with constructions of the social world. Instantly, we can make connections back to a Bourdieuian analysis of domestic space and the shaping of desire to purchase and consume this highly particular architectural form.

Drawing upon this poststructural critique of Modernity and capitalism we can identify a process whereby the presumptions that underpin the notion of oedipus have been, via the narrative of the nuclear family, internalized into habitus. Oedipus, in this reading, is a descriptor for the symbolic violence which takes place within the Modernist nuclear family. Social narratives and institutions that base their legitimacy around an oedipal symbolic violence are acting to restrain and redirect individual trajectories along prescribed pathways—a particular capitalist habitus is inculcated in relation to the norms of oedipus. These norms, these practices, beliefs, desires, are linked fundamentally to the cycle of capitalist production within the era of the nationstate. Oedipus, in this analysis, is constitutive of an historical moment in the evolution of capitalism and acts to create specific types of subjectivities, identities and physical bodies. Marcuse (1956) identifies the totalitarianism of contemporary civilization, suggesting that each of us is kept in a "state of permanent mobilization, internal and external" (p. 93). Habermas (1973) also developed this notion of ongoing crises within capitalism. This relates well to the concept of the axiomatic flow of capitalism. The point here is that the oedipal oscillation set up within the nuclear family narrative (which we can draw from Wilden's work), and which extends into the relationship between each individual and larger social institutions, acts to maintain this mobilization and the fundamental binary habitus formations which allow it. Thus, once we accept the oedipalized relationships and social position of the nuclear family, we are also accepting the binarist epistemology and the distributions of social power they represent.

That is why the nuclear family *is* oedipus *is* double bind.

Accept the nuclear family and the reality it represents as a given and the whole of your world shifts into a binary schema. Thus, oedipus becomes a machine of symbolic violence[16]. And yet, a critical analysis such as this cannot end here. Processes of symbolic violence, as Bourdieu has argued, are linked to broader

---

[16]   For an explication of Bourdieu's sociological framework, including the key concepts of habitus and symbolic violence, see Carrington & Luke (1997).

political agendas. In the case of Western societies the various forms of capitalism have shaped these agendas, and consequently, cannot be separated from the processes of symbolic violence and embodiment identified here. The nuclear narrative actively participates in this political agenda.

Within his ecosystemic framing, Wilden would see the family as the site and source of relationships which result in the colonization of the individual[17]. For Wilden, this colonization is but one part of a bigger picture that includes us all. We are all colonized, and the nuclear family is a primary site of this action, an ideological and physical site where our habitus is formed in particular oedipalized ways. Deleuze and Guattari also note the imperialism which takes place—"we are all little colonies and it is Oedipus that colonizes us" (1983, p. 264)—displaying a shared understanding that each of us are absorbed within the capitalist relation, that the specific characteristics of habitus are moulded by the repressions of desire which constitute oedipalization. Explicating this further, Seem (1983, p. xx) writes that, "Oedipus is the figurehead of imperialism, colonization pursued by other means, it is the interior colony....it is our intimate colonial education".

Thus, oedipus represents perhaps the fundamental symbolic violence of our culture within nationstate capitalism in its imposition of a cultural system and way of being in the world without connecting these practices and values to "the power relations which are at their source" (Bourdieu & Passeron 1990, p. 41). And, it takes place within the nuclear family. It constitutes a very particular form of symbolic violence, one that focuses on the construction of particular familial identities and relationships within a particular historical juncture. Other processes of symbolic violence, all of which act to constitute particular symbolic systems, build upon this primary colonization, this intimate association with the fundamental normative principles of this moment of capitalism. The term 'endocolonization' has been used by Massumi (1992) to focus the processes of colonization into domestic space and the family. To begin, Massumi refutes the family narrative of closure and privacy:

> The family is not a closed microcosm, even if it is represented and represents itself as one. It opens directly onto the social field. A body does not grow up sheltered from society, enclosed in the family that feeds it. Rather, the family opens the body to society's feeding itself off it (1992, p. 81).

Massumi's point here is that the family constructs exploitable subjectivities and bodies. The family is not, in this analysis, a safe sanctuary from the trials of public life. He goes on to further describe the function of the nuclear family in terms of value relationships where the socius produces particular bodies in order to 'feed' off them:

---

[17]   Wilden (1987) describes this as the 'Cinderella Complex' where women are secretly fearful of independence and wait in hope for a Prince Charming to arrive and rescue them from all responsibility. He writes of the 'colonial rule' which creates the enabling circumstances for this condition. See also, Dowling (1981).

> The family is a device for the capture of bodily potential (channelization) by social
> forces of domination dedicated to the vampiric extraction of surplus value and the cyclic
> resupply of the bodies from which this surplus value is sucked (p. 81).

The relationships of the nuclear family become processes of symbolic violence, acting to construct particular politicized realities and bodily positionings. In this reading, oedipus is the route to the reproduction of this vampiric cycle—it constructs willing victims. And the particular types of victims constructed are those essential to the maintenance of the existing society—consumers.

To account for the apparent success of this oedipalizing system of symbolic violence, Wilden argues that not only are we colonized, but also we are taught to desire this colonization:

> ...the strategy of domination teaches the colonized to prefer their oppressors to
> themselves...it teaches the privileged to blame the victims for their plight, and ...teaches
> the victims to blame each other (1987, p. 47).

The nuclear family and the processes it represents, then, act to shape our desire, to colonize us. There is a cycle of colonization and oppression identified by Wilden, who continues:

> when the victims come to believe that they suffer because they 'really' are (inherently
> or genetically) inferior or because they deserve what they get...then the circle of
> destruction is complete. One is collaborating in one's own oppression (p. 47).

This may sound too much like conspiracy theory, however, Wilden and Massumi are attempting to destroy any claim to neutrality that might be made on behalf of the nuclear family narrative. By this account, the nuclear family is a site which, rather than protecting and enriching, refracts processes of symbolic violence. It is via the symbolic violence of this familial 'endocolonization' that the habitus takes on its specific characteristics.

Key here is the recognition that we are programmed to desire in particular ways and to participate within this cycle of repression and domination. One of the mechanisms of oedipalization within this narrative—the oscillations of double bind form the cornerstone of Wilden's understandings of nationstate capitalism.

Oedipus and double bind

Both Wilden and the Deleuze-Guattari collaborations draw upon Gregory Bateson's (1972)[18] notions of double bind. Rather than a choice between unsavoury alternatives, a no-win situation, double bind "requires a choice between two states, each of which are equally valued and so equally insufficient that a self-perpetuating oscillation is engendered by any act of choice between them" (Wilden & Wilson 1976, p. 276). Two messages are given simultaneously, both are equally valued

---

[18]   Bateson (1972) developed the notion of the double bind in relation to his studies of the relationship
        between schizophrenia, family, and communication. See also, Watzlawick, Beavan & Jackson
        (1967).

(Bateson 1972; Deleuze & Guattari 1983), and yet one message denies the other (Weakland 1976). And, while the need to choose is created by the context in which the double bind is embedded, the inability to make a choice, to come to a resolution, is also created. As Weakland (1976) describes it, there is no avenue for metacommunication about the messages or their content.

Turning to the nuclear family, inherent in the choices set up within the oedipalized family is the opposition, which Deleuze and Guattari theorized, between oedipus and schizophrenia. Here, oedipus represents a moral code and normative reality dictated and maintained within a Modernist nationstate paradigm that is in turn premised upon the reality of an integrated and unitary identity. Schizophrenia, on the other hand, represents the refusal of this moral code. Each message denies the other. The alternate realities of schizophrenics represent a challenge to normed reality, of which nuclear family is key. Ongoing processes of symbolic violence ensure that habitus are constructed to recognize the legitimacy of this choice, to share the valuations of normed behaviour versus schizophrenic behaviour. To appreciate the normative power of this constructed polemic, a more detailed understanding of schizophrenia is required.

Oedipus and schizophrenia

A problematization of oedipus necessarily problematizes schizophrenia. Both are unmasked as mutually reinforcing normative agendas linked to particular narratives of self, family and nation. Schizophrenia has become a feared 'social' disease, assuming the same role as literacy and juvenile crime as markers of the relative health of society. Western society, via the practices of specialized, delegated and professionalized clinicians, has invoked clinical schizophrenia to describe—in effect, to recapture and punish—those who have unsuccessfully challenged the context of the oedipal paradox. These polemic constructions have set the outer limits of normalized behaviour in Modernist society. When used in this way, the presence of schizophrenics points to a breakdown of the normative agenda in particular families, a glitch in the inculcation of particular oedipalized realities.

Referring back to Wilden's communicational frame, we could say, then, that the schizophrenic's coding system differs in fundamental aspects from that of the larger socius. Traditional psychoanalysis and clinical practice have interpreted this mismatch of codes, or competing realities, in terms of individual dysfunction, drawing particularly upon notions of the unitary individual and a unified identity. Deleuze and Guattari offer us an alternative framing which does not rest upon a premise of fundamental unity, distinguishing between schizophrenia as an attempt to escape the effects of particular social machines and what they term 'clinical schizophrenia'. For them schizophrenia is not a pathological condition, rather, the loss of reality associated with schizophrenia may be the result of forced oedipalization more than it is an outcome of the schizophrenic process (1983).

The general distaste felt in relation to this apparent refusal of oedipus, wholeness and incorporation into the dominant reality is the response of those made to see that the world in which they live and in which they have major libidinal and economic investments, may not be the only one available. The existence of schizophrenia calls into question the rationality of the mainstream—if it is so self-evident, why are some of us sent 'mad' by it?—undermining the prevailing epistemology and the boundaries it institutes. A cynical view would argue that the value of schizophrenia as a cautionary tale depends on the existence of example cases; therefore, as one mechanism in the maintenance of the nuclear narrative, schizophrenics are produced. Here again, it is clear that oedipus and schizophrenia are differing positions along the same normative continuum. Ominously, Deleuze and Guattari write of oedipus "tying off the unconscious on both sides", and of its increasing danger if people begin to question it: "then the cops are there to replace the high priests" (1983, p. 81). The high priests they mention are, of course, psychoanalysts as institutional authorities. Here, Deleuze and Guattari are tacitly making reference to the total connection between the nuclear family narrative and the disciplines which flow out of it, and the maintenance of existing power hierarchies. In this view, psychoanalysts are instrumental in these politically loaded categorizations. One such disciplinary tactic, is the shifting delineation of mental disorder.

Schizophrenia was originally known as "dementia preacox"—dementia of early life—because it was generally deemed to have an onset in early adulthood, and was first identified and labelled by Kraeplin in 1896. Bleuler later renamed the condition "schizophrenia" to highlight the fracture between thinking and feeling which he identified in sufferers (Warner 1985). Schizophrenia is generally understood as an illness, and its diagnosis involves the identification of a number of symptoms including "auditory hallucinations, bizarre and irrational beliefs, disordered thought as manifest in incoherent speech, poverty of affect, and social withdrawal" (Bentall 1990, p. xi). Clinical schizophrenia, then, is understood to be a syndrome identifiable by the presence of a number of symptoms. However, the schizophrenic population which was identified by Kraeplin and Bleuler bears little resemblance to contemporary accounts of schizophrenia (Boyle 1990). What these men called schizophrenia would not be recognized as such today. Here, note that delineations of mental disorder are, at best, arbitrary. Foucault (1973, 1979, 1986a, 1986b) and Szasz (1974, 1994) identified the matrix of power within which shifting boundaries of mental health and illness are positioned.

As fundamental to modern psychiatry as the term has been, a number of problems with the concept of schizophrenia have been identified. Bentall (1990, p. xiii) notes that:

> serious questions remain about whether schizophrenia can be considered an 'illness' about whether it is one condition or several; about whether clear dividing lines can be found between schizophrenia and normal functioning or even between schizophrenia and other kinds of mental disorder.

Additionally, it would appear in hindsight, that Bleuler and Kraeplin allowed their own versions of normality to influence their identification of the various syndromes and precursors of schizophrenia (Boyle 1990). Thus the diagnosis and treatment of schizophrenia has always been a normative and politically loaded activity, demonstrated by the fact that there are very few aspects of human behaviour that have not, at some time, been linked to the aetiology of schizophrenia (Bentall 1990).

The social potency of schizophrenia is reflected in the application of this label to one per cent of the population of Western countries at some point in their lives, leading to social marginalization, exposure to "powerful medications", and movement in and out of psychiatric institutions (Bentall 1990). Boyle (1990) goes so far as to argue that Bleuler and Kraepelin did not discover anything and, in fact, misdiagnosed other conditions. To sum up the general obscurity of the schizophrenic concept, Bentall notes that:

> Given that schizophrenia appears to be a disorder with no particular symptoms, no particular course, no particular outcome, and which responds to no particular treatment, it is unsurprising that 100 years of research has failed to establish that is has any particular cause" (1990, pp. 32-33).

This failure to isolate a cause, appropriate treatment or to agree on classic symptoms allows the possibility of a link to the role of schizophrenia as a mechanism for control, working in concert with the symbolic violence of oedipus. The labelling of an individual as schizophrenic becomes a social label of marginalization and alienation, virtually guaranteeing a career on the outskirts of society. In the West in particular, schizophrenics experience more extensive social devaluation than either criminals or the 'retarded' (Warner 1985). It seems that the status of schizophrenia in many ways mirrors that of the oedipus complex. In effect, they are co-dependent concepts. Schizophrenia is positioned in Western society as the evil twin, the binary opposite of oedipus. Where oedipus represents contained ego boundaries and a unified reality (stability control and normalcy), schizophrenia is associated with unstable, multiple realities and eroded ego boundaries—a loss of control, judged by oedipal standards. We are caught between the two, fearful of moving too far in either direction: the oedipal double bind and the nuclear family.

Not for the fainthearted, then. Schizophrenia is a potent concept. Regardless of its disputed existence as a disease, it is a very powerful social signifier which, once assigned to an individual, destines him or her to continued marginalization and negative social sanction. This label is applied if and when the individual strays in any substantive way from the norms established via the symbolic violence of oedipus.

Returning to the link between this normative dualism and the family, the question becomes, what is the mechanism which has kept us within the confines of the nuclear family narrative? The answer is the oedipal relationship. Oedipus—our capture within it—is achieved and maintained via the unresolved double bind. The oedipal relation which *is* the nuclear family *is* an ongoing double bind, keeping us trapped within it until such time as we contest the context or the larger context itself alters. As we have seen in relation to the diagnosis of schizophrenia, individual contestation is fraught with risk—risk of social exclusion and sanction. In the process of normal psychosexual development as envisaged by Freud, the child must desire the parent and must then refuse to gratify this basic instinct, sublimating it for the good of the greater social order[19]. For Freud:

> it is impossible to overlook the extent to which civilization is built up upon a renunciation of instinct, how much it presupposes precisely the non-satisfaction (by suppression, repression or some other means?) of powerful instincts (1995, p. 742).

This forced shaping of sexual desire established the pattern of relationships which constitute the nuclear family within Fordist capitalism. Make no mistake, this was a specific narrative matched to a specific historical moment.

By this account, the repression of desire, which Freud understood in terms of the dissolution of the Oedipus complex[20], laid the groundwork for an ongoing series of desire-repression cycles which controlled and channelled powerful human instincts. And as Sprengnether (1995) pointed out, simultaneously ascribed gender and culture. Here, the suppression and repression Freud (1995) identified as essential to civilization depends on a view of desire as an instinct barely kept under control, as something which has the potential for harm on an individual and societal level. Uncontrolled desire is constructed as a personal weakness, as a boundary between normal and pathological.

Guilt, alienation and hostility are constant companions in this equation. This is what Wilden identified as the colonization of the individual within capitalism—the individual is constructed to *desire* the repression and alienation of her desires. Thus, desire is represented as an ultimately negative force and it was this construction that Deleuze and Guattari challenged. The normative dynamic between desire and repression sets up a series of unresolvable choices, thereby capturing family members within the ensuing oscillation. The processes of symbolic violence *construct* repressed and unfulfilled desire, guilt and anger and represent it as normal development within the safety of the nuclear family. Freud, further, took this repression of instinct and desire as the model for the development of human culture, linking the nuclear family, the site of the oedipal colonization, to the foundation and continuation of Western civilization (Marcuse 1956). Marcuse argues that:

> The concept of man that emerges from Freudian theory is the most irrefutable indictment of Western civilization—and at the same time the most unshakable defense of this civilization. According to Freud, the history of man is the history of his

---

[19] As an interesting and not unrelated aside, the child is portrayed as somehow complicit in the progress of this relationship, leaving us with a development agenda reeking of essentialist understandings of childhood and the universalization of a particular cultural and historically placed notion of childhood and child/human development.

[20] It is necessary for normal development, Freud argues (1995, p. 663-664) that the individual "turn away" from the Oedipus complex. In so doing, girls substitute the desire for a penis for desire for a baby; boys turn away to avoid castration. Girls turn towards motherhood, boys towards markers of masculine identity.

repression. Culture constrains not only his societal but also his biological existence, not only parts of the human being but his instinctual structure itself (1956, p. 11).

The role of oedipus and the nuclear family in all this has been to *code* desire, to create a particular habitus, and thus biologic and instinctual, framework. This framing is negative, conceptualizing desire as a force which must be contained in order to maintain a stable society. Against Freud, Deleuze and Guattari are adamant that desire is active—it produces, it is a dynamic open system. Freud's Oedipus has reduced desire to the status of a constructed social relation where desire *becomes* libido *becomes* the oedipal relation, remaining unresolved and trapped within the family triangle. In this reading, the oedipal nuclear family is complicit in construction of particular cycles of desire and repression necessary to the maintenance of Fordist capitalism.

Deleuze and Guattari (1983) argue quite clearly that oedipus is neither innate nor originary. Rather, it is the pivotal act of symbolic violence in our society. Further, this framing suggests that the nuclear family narrative acts to inculcate in individuals, habitus schemata that then predispose the continuation of this unresolved oscillation. The nuclear family, as mythologized in Western doctrine, is a social mechanism that regulates, creates paradox, codes. This view problematizes the apolitical framing of nuclear family as the endpoint of social evolution. By this account, the nuclear, oedipalized family is the site *par excellence* of systemic symbolic violence. And not just any symbolic violence but rather the inculcation of a systematic framework of values and beliefs and sanctions which mirror the requirements of capitalism.

There is a connection, then, between the oedipalized citizen and a particular phase of capitalism. The repressions and desires which are inculcated via the symbolic violence of oedipus act to connect us to the processes of nationstate capitalism. While desire was explicitly contained and shaped within the double bind of familial relationships, capital value was attached to production and thus solidly grounded. Thus, within nationstate capitalism, capital was firmly linked to production: Fordist economics was constructed so that individual consumption was directly tied to individual production and the market value. As Habermas, Chomsky and Marcuse argued, we are constructed to desire our own domination. As well, we are constructed to desire commodities—to virtually identify self in line with our ability to consume goods and experiences. Wilden's (1980) ecosystemic framing recognizes the bridge between desire[21], and the unitary individual as the core of the mind/body split and all else which has followed, including the alienation of humankind from production on one hand and from ecological awareness on the other. Trapped as it is within the symbolic violence of oedipus, this notion of desire is the nexus around which modern Western society, both knowingly and unknowingly, revolves.

---

[21] Wilden draws his understandings of desire and of psychoanalysis in general from his work as Lacan's English translator.

Conclusion

Let me review the basic tenets of Deleuze and Guattari's argument. Oedipus has been unproblematically viewed as innate, and this acceptance has led to a large edifice of theory which is premised upon normative notions of identity and social practice. To demonstrate its role as a primary normative mechanism, rather than an innate characteristic, Deleuze and Guattari (1983) made the connection between oedipus and schizophrenia. For them, oedipus is a "figure of power" (Seem 1983, p. xx) and schizophrenia is one manoeuvre in the use of this power. Psychoanalysis, in this view, is a tool of colonization and domination in its reduction of all human desire and activity to the oedipal family. Schizophrenia is the condition of loss of ego, and the construction and maintenance of ego is at the core of oedipus—the primary symbolic violence of our society. This understanding of individual and boundaried 'self' that is internalised and set apart from the body and from the outside world is a key characteristic of modern philosophy and psychology. This is why the social sanctions against schizophrenia are so extreme and long-lasting. The schizophrenic subverts the boundaries of identity and social practice established through the symbolic violence of oedipus. The bottom line here is that the symbolic violence of oedipus actively conspires in the construction of a particular type of citizen—one whose habitus is in tune with the needs of nationstate capitalism and the social and political forms it spawned.

Given the position of influence gained by psychology and psychiatry in our society during the twentieth century, this is a powerful critique. It calls into questions one of the fundamental framing concepts for the ways in which we have perceived ourselves and our society. If we take this view, the family becomes the social and physical space where the deeply ingrained colonization takes place. This is a highly politicized account of family, very distant from the neutral family of apolitical approaches.

The critiques developed by Bourdieu, Wilden and Deleuze and Guattari all emerged from within Modernism. They were attempts to understand the processes that created the Modern individual within a particular moment in the history of capitalism. The conceptual schemes developed by Deleuze and Guattari, Bourdieu and Wilden provide a useful theoretical position in their ability to reveal the principles of normativity operant within existing sociocultural and economic circumstances. However, these frameworks emerged from within a particular historical phase—nationstate capitalism—and as a consequence are constrained by patterns of presence and absence specific to this form of capitalism. For these theorists, then, ethnicity and culture were still viewed as organically binding categories. While identifying the normative project of nationstate capitalism they nevertheless had no insight into the impact of epochal shifts in capitalism on issues of identity and subjectivity and the other accounting systems of that society such as ethnicity, sexuality and race. That is, in this regard they are Modernist theories *par excellence*—tied to broad paradigmatic assumptions about *inter alia*, nationstate, economics and race. All three theoretical projects identified capitalism as the defining characteristic of human existence in modern Western societies. While Bourdieu may dispute this interpretation of his work and argue instead that his framework is universally applicable, his understanding of market economy, the differing forms of capital and the emphasis he applies to the operation of symbolic violence are all drawn from the cultural experience of mid-twentieth century capitalism.

The role of the nuclear family narrative in the inculcation of Modernist mindsets and the operation of capitalism has been foregrounded by each account. Rather than the safe, closed haven from public life identified by traditional sociological and social psychological approaches to the family, these critiques identified the complicity of the nuclear narrative in the symbolic violence and repression which made possible Modernist capitalism and the nationstate. Deleuze and Guattari, particularly, identify the collusion of major Modernist discourses such as psychoanalysis and psychology in the control of individuals and larger populations. No longer an innocent, natural formation, the family has become politicized. It is almost as though these critiques constitute a self-created oppositional position to apolitical theories of traditional family sociology and economics. These framings have identified the pivotal nature of the nuclear family narrative as the mode of inculcating and measuring the normative principles of this particular stage of capitalist society.

The set of Chapters in Part One have historicized approaches to family. Each of the ways in which we have chosen to analyze family in our society are historically and culturally mediated. Structural Functionalism and Systems Theory emerged in the post-war years of aggressive American hegemony and their view of family reflects the ideological and economic agendas of the time. Critical Theory emerged in counterpoint, from a different philosophical context. The power of the nuclear family narrative is obvious here—regardless of framing, it is the *monocultural nuclear family* that is viewed as 'normal' and, as Deleuze and Guattari demonstrate, this normalizing process is deeply entrenched in the narratives of our culture. Bourdieu's articulation of symbolic violence provides a vocabulary for unpacking the impact of these narratives.

In Part Two, we move outside a focus on the family. Over the last 15-20 years we have experienced an escalating and rapid change in key economic and social structures. If we are to understand family in the new century it is important to contextualize it. The next set of Chapters, then, outlines the changes that have overtaken western society and begins to trace their impact for family.

PART TWO

FROM FORDIST-KEYNESIANISM TO NEOLIBERAL NEW ECONOMIES

The worst error of all is to suppose that capitalism is simply an economic system (Braudel 1985, p. 623).

CHAPTER 5

THE BOOM YEARS: 1945-1973

INTRODUCTION

Given the underlying premise of this text—that there is a fundamental and complex connection between economic, political and social systems---it is appropriate to overview the trajectory of capitalism since the end of World War Two. This is particularly important since I have tracked the entrenchment of the nuclear narrative to this historical moment. I begin with the period, 1945-1973. For most commentators, be they economic, international relations, postcolonial or globalization theorists, there is a recognizable divide between the period from World War Two through to the end of the post-war boom—the years between 1945 and 1973—and the post-1973 period. It was during the initial post-war boom years that the 'modern' world took shape, demonstrating what could be described as a reterritorialization of both nationspace and personspace.

The post-war world divided itself along political and economic axes as the movement towards decolonization gathered momentum and these new nations were added to the cauldron of international economic and security agreements. This was the period when the International Monetary Fund (IMF), the United Nations and the World Bank were established, along with collective security blocs based around treaties such as ANZUS and NATO in the West and the Warsaw Pact in the East. This reformation of physical, ideological and financial boundaries in the wake of World War Two was accompanied by the de- and reterritorialization of ethnicities and nationalisms as individuals and groups were reshaped according to the new-look post-war globe.

These were not free-flowing changes in identity. Rather, these newly forming nations and ethnic identifications became part of the stakes played for during the Cold War (Leys 1996) as opposing ideological positions attempted to make territorial and political gains. In this climate, national and ethnic identity were politically charged constructs, which played a role in the international balance of power. They represented powerful forces of symbolic violence, which were played out in a newly emergent global arena. Consider briefly the case of women in post-war Western nations. As one aspect of the creation of homogeneous national identity and economic power, gender roles were actively reconstituted: men returned from war service and women, who had been constructed as capable and independent workers for the nation during the war years, were recast as homemakers and mothers to make way for male employment. Within the space of a very few years, women were constructed as capable workers/partners and then suddenly reconstructed as dependent homemakers and wives. A vigorous process of inculcation via mass media, education and governmental policy came into play in order to enforce this transition—an example of the potency of processes of symbolic violence. A significant part of this transition focused around the idea of the nuclear family: this narrative acted to provide roles for men and women in a time of readjustment and change. And this process took place nowhere more efficiently than in the United States.

NATION BUILDING

America emerged from the Second World War as the pre-eminent military and economic power in the world. Not only did it emerge with major industrial infrastructure intact and booming, but it was also the only nation to command a demonstrated nuclear weapons capability. As Reifer and Sudler (1996) point out, the achievement of nuclear weapons capacity was a defining moment in the history of American political, economic and cultural hegemony. Nuclear capacity was a seemingly irrefutable demonstration of the dominance of logical positivism, legitimizing the co-option of legitimate 'knowledge production' by the United States, particularly its assertion of hegemonic cultural and scientific-cum-technical power in the closing stages of the Second World War[22]. The American venture into space was unparalleled as a publicity event, but it had the additional effect of focusing prolonged world attention on the technological and moral superiority of the USA. On the ideological battlefields of the Cold War era, America was sending a clear message about its cultural and moral strength—this was an America united, strong, and with a clear technological and economic advantage.

As importantly, the United States emerged from the War and the immediate post-war period with a sense of its own potential—with a clear understanding of its role within the emerging global political process. It then used its military and economic might to underwrite American cultural and ideological hegemony and the world divided into a bipolar Cold War order centering around the USA and the USSR. This global intervention was constructed as the moral obligation of a superior cultural and economic power within the parameters of Modernization Theory—which "represented the effort of Western social science (in the light of the Cold War and the political drive for national liberation) to come to grips with a world which included the non-Western and the non-rich" (Lee 1996, p. 181).

This world-view was, and for many remains, heavily colored by Social Darwinism whereby 'development' was directed to a distant and superior endpoint—in this case, Westernized industrial society—towards which all other economic and social systems would ultimately move. In this view, a linear progression from 'traditional'

---

[22]   The United States repeatedly demonstrated its technological superiority over its allied partners and the Germans and Japanese, for example, in the mass manufacture and distribution of warships, aircraft and small arms weapons culminating in the use of atomic weapons to end the war in the Pacific.

to 'modern' democratic societies could be traced. This ultimately ideological framing drew directly from Structural Functionalism (Leys 1996) to the point of assuming an apolitical status for itself. From this moral and epistemological position the excesses of capitalism, and those who represented it, could be excused as inevitable in the overall scheme of the natural progression of world societies towards the Western ideal. Not all, of course, applauded the technological and cultural changes taking place. As we have seen, Wilden (1980) argued insistently that belief in the unlimited natural progress of capitalism was an ideological misrecognition of the actual limits of this system while the theorists of the Frankfurt Institute were watchful of the social impacts. Third World Marxists were also critical of the outcomes of this developing economic and cultural hegemony for their own nations (see, for example, Cardosa 1972; Frank 1991; Palma 1978).

Criticisms aside, these parallel strands bound themselves into a very neat and effective package, made all the more effective by economic restructuring and the processes of decolonization which the European colonial powers were undergoing. Given our own recent experiences of the fall of the Soviet bloc, it is here, in this brief moment of instability, that we might expect to locate the contemporary embryonic emergence of new ethnicities. However, instead of an historical moment in which multiple ethnic identifications might find a legitimate space, what emerged was the spread of a particular homogenizing understanding of the modern world— an international process of symbolic violence which constructed the world in terms of the Cold War, Modernization Theory and requirements of Fordist capitalism. While new nations emerged during this time, each of these was born at the expense of diversity. Processes of symbolic violence accompanied by overt political forces constructed, in each nation, a homogeneous national identity that was portrayed to the international society of nations. In this climate, internal ethnic and even individual diversity was effectively silenced.

Of paramount importance to the players in this new and exciting game of Cold War politics was the internal stability and strength of the nationstate entity. Where ethnicity and cultural difference were recognized, it was in the form of multiculturalism, itself a Modernist accounting of difference. In a multicultural rendering of cultural diversity, the dominant host society was never challenged to the point of change and cultural difference was minimized in relation to larger national discourses which reflected the imperatives of boundary maintenance in the face of outside menace (Featherstone 1993). Subcultural differences, for example intermarriage or interethnicity, were rendered invisible by the limited vocabulary and ideological space available at this time for foregrounding them. This focus on external threat and the associated need for internal coherence and strength is noted by Featherstone (1993, p. 173):

> As nation states become increasingly drawn together in a tighter figuration of competing nations, they faced strong pressures to develop a coherent cultural identity. The process of the homogenization of culture, the project of creating a common culture, must be understood as a process in the unification of culture of the need to ignore, or at best synthesize and blend, local differences. Yet the process of formation of such a

culture cannot be understood merely as a response to forces within the nation state, but must also be seen in relation to forces outside of it: the potential for the development of national identity and cultural coherence as relationally determined by the structure of the shifting dis-equilibriums of power and interdependencies of the figuration of nation states which a particular country was embedded.

Featherstone is here marking the process of national identity building which took place alongside the delineation of separate nationstates. Note also the significance of international forces—a perception of international instability or threat creates strong pressures for national unity, interpreted as cultural homogeneity. This has not, of course, been an isolated historical moment. Rather, nations have emerged and disappeared throughout history, and modern nationstate boundaries have been redefined a number of times over the last few generations. Alongside these shifts have been movements amongst the ranks of inclusion and exclusion within these states.

The construction and reconstruction of ethnic identities within normalized parameters and the accompanying processes of inclusion and exclusion have been a crucial ingredient of nation-building. Indonesia is an example of this: post-war internal politics mitigated towards a fear of communists and, as a direct result, ethnic Chinese were immediately suspect (Vervoorn 1998). Fiji has just resumed elections in the wake of the latest coup—an election which, reflecting ongoing ethnic unrest, returned the Fijian-Indian dominated political party but which also elected the most recent failed coup leader from his jail cell. As well, countries such as Burma, India and Pakistan, where whole ethnic populations were pitted against each other to the advantage of British and Dutch colonial rule, have experienced ongoing ethnic conflict in the wake of this period of colonialism. Emphasis, in the new nuclear age, was on citizenship and race and nuclear family, and culture was discursively constructed in national terms. Where ethnicity was ascribed, it was used as an exclusionary discourse to marginalize various groups (for example, the Jews, diasporic Asian groups, European gypsies, guest workers) whose presence was believed to potentially destablilize the strength of a unified nation.

Structural Functionalism as a mode of social inquiry has been particularly aligned with this US intellectual and technological hegemony. It adopted an acritical view of the legitimacy of the post-war capitalist economic system, accepting it as an ahistorical and self-evident reality. Taking up this theme, Habermas (1973) suggested that the democratic *polis*, with its equal and unitary, yet ultimately non-participatory citizenry, encouraged the seeming "naturalness" of a capitalist society. Functionalism's apolitical position with its connection to classical physics and visions of the nuclear family as the corner stone of advanced societies underwrote these notions, becoming one link in the legitimation process which surrounded US cultural and economic hegemony. It is the taken-for-granted realities that are the most potent symbolic violences. What took place, then, was a reterritorialization and recoding of knowledge around specific types of technology, undoubtedly accompanied by shifts in the production of particular subjectivities and cultural narratives—in effect, Functionalism constituted a technology of domination. In this it was complicit in a process of symbolic violence which acted to construct a particular type of ideal citizen. The human face of this phase of US hegemony was a discourse of sociocultural homogeneity. Ethnic identifications were subsumed within discourses of nationhood, and racial difference was in turn subsumed, unsuccessfully, within the rhetoric of technological advancement and international relations. This, then, was a highly politicized and historically situated construction of identity and the social world.

One of the earliest and most striking social critiques of post-World War Two capitalism was developed by Herbert Marcuse. Marcuse railed against the aggressive dominance of positivist science and technology. For him, it led to a lessening of the human condition and the narrowing of the potentiality of each life. Of particular interest are the links Marcuse made between Freudian theories of the individual and her integration into, and control within, capitalism. Capitalist society, Marcuse argued, drawing upon Freudian theories of the relationship between repression and civilization, demanded a greater repression of the individual than was required for the maintenance of the society itself. Freud required an individual who repressed sexual pleasure and other human instincts in order to fit into and contribute to, society (Marcuse 1956). For Marcuse, the multiple repressions which were reaching an apogee in the twentieth century went beyond what was required to achieve a coherent culture. In *One Dimensional Man*, he argues that:

> The distinguishing feature of advanced industrial society is its effective suffocation of those needs which demand liberation—liberation also from that which is tolerable and rewarding and comfortable—while it sustains and absolves the destructive power and repressive function of the affluent society. Here, the social controls exact the overwhelming need for the production and consumption of waste; the need for stupefying work where it is no longer a real necessity; the needs for modes of relaxation which soothe and prolong this stupefication; the need for maintaining such deceptive liberties as free competition at administered prices, a free press which censors itself, free choice between brands and gadgets (Marcuse 1964, p. 7).

A sad indictment of modern industrial society: a place where everything, including our sense of ourselves, is manufactured and consumed and cushioned. With this sentiment, Marcuse foreshadowed the poststructuralist philosophies of Deleuze-Guattari as well as describing the underlying conditions which made possible the Keynesian social contract. Prominent amongst the social institutions which manufactured and imposed these repressions was the family—a family which drew legitimacy for its normative shape and function within Modernist capitalism directly from the oedipal-directed and phallocentric theories of Freud.

Like Marcuse, Habermas has noted the ability of capitalist societies to remove the will of the population for radical change. While all citizens are represented within political rhetoric and mainstream social narratives as equal participants in the processes of decision-making and political participation, non-participatory democracy has become the hallmark of capitalist societies (Habermas 1973). Chomsky (1999) makes the same observations in his critiques of modern democracies. We each have the illusion of participation in the politics of state, but in reality, we are marginalized and controlled via normative narratives, of which the integrated individual and the nuclear family have been key.

THE KEYNESIAN SOCIAL CONTRACT

The particular relationship between a Fordist economy, homogeneous nationstate and the ideal citizen-worker constructed within these normative narratives was exemplified in what became known as the Keynesian social contract. This time frame is often referred to as Fordist-Keynesian in an attempt to capture the connection between the economic, political and social which emerged during this time. 'Fordism' as a term denotes the post-war boom years, roughly between 1945 and 1973, paralleling what Lee (1996) has identified as the rise of positivism and a sense of satisfaction with the status quo (Kellner 1984). Ford, the man, was a major pioneer of mass production techniques and the payment of high enough base wages to male workers to encourage employee retention (the cost of training workers for the production line was high) and a production-consumption cycle—the axis of the Keynesian social contract—where consumption was driven by production. Effectively, the Keynesian model is an equilibrium model, where economic and social balance is maintained via the practices of state intervention in the form of monetary and trade regulation and a burgeoning web of welfare initiatives. The underside of this was the deskilling of the entire blue-collar workforce as each worker became but one exchangeable cog in a larger assembly line, the subjectification of all workers to an industrial temporal and spatial rhythm, and a reterritorialization of home/work boundaries and gender divisions. Accompanying this was a system of state sanctioned constructions of appropriate parenting, visions of childhood, sexuality and an increasing role for government in the legitimation of social activity. These were facilitated by the range of apolitical family theorizations identified earlier. In this light, the Keynesian social contract reveals itself as a mutually reinforcing system of symbolic violences. A system ultimately policed, Deleuze and Guattari (1983) argued, by the use of schizophrenia as a final normative boundary for intransigents who would not or who could not conform to the requirements of a Keynesian social and moral order.

The role of consumption

During this relative boom time of high male employment and rising living standards in the post-war victor states, consumption became a social norm and the workers, in Marcuse's words, were contained and stifled within the "comfortable, smooth, reasonable, democratic unfreedom" (1964, p. 1). Marcuse is essentially arguing that the workers were taught to desire their own domination, and this domination served as a transformer which absorbed and fuelled the growth of production. Production drove consumption, rather than vice versa. In a Fordist economy, the ideal citizen-worker became a conspicuous consumer. An individual's or family's upward social mobility was marked by their acquisition of consumer goods. Women, in particular, were targeted for the consumption of home products and fashion, and shopping became increasingly a marker of taste, a performative art, rather than a necessity. In the immediate post-war period, then, women in the industrialized West, were aggressively reconstructed as mothers and homemakers and then once again as commodity consumers.

Interestingly, what emerges here is an epistemological division created between production and consumption, related to the genesis of our use and understanding of the concepts of Marxist class theory. An interesting gender dynamic arises here also—while the men of this time period were aggressively constructed as producers, women were appointed to the opposing role of consumers. This paralleled the division set up between public and private spaces, between work and home, between men's work and women's work. Although more recent commentators have tended to position them along a continuum (see, for example, Touraine 1995), there has, nevertheless, continued to be a tendency to differentiate between production and consumption (Webster 1995)—a conceptualization which positions them as unitary and static categories, in the same way as identity, gender and culture were taken to be fixed. Given the sense of the axiomatic developed by Dclcuzc and Guattari we would have to argue that there can be no divide nor opposition nor static positioning between these two concepts: without consumption, there can be no production; without production there will be no consumption. They are part of the same 'flow'. Wilden, also, would dispute such an oppositional rendering of these processes. For Wilden, they would represent differing logical types, that is, differing organizational levels within a hierarchical order. However, his enduring concern was to illustrate the inversion of real, ecosystemic relationships constructed and maintained by capitalist doctrine, and I therefore believe that his focus would be on exposing the ideological screen which had obscured our understanding of the real relationship between these two processes. Wilden's explanatory framework would recognize the incorporation of smaller systems, or subsystems, within the larger 'supersystem' of capitalism. His interest in the production-consumption relation would be based in the ideological misrecognition of connections between the two.

The politicized nature of the Fordist-Keynesian relation which an ecosystemic analysis reveals, has not gone unremarked. Massumi (1997a) argues that the Keynesian social contract which established this supply-and-demand relationship was an attempt to 'internalize' the outside threat of worker revolution or the internal threat of overproduction into the day-to-day operations of capitalism. For Massumi, the imperatives of Keynesianism are apparent:

> Social equilibrium was to be attained by integrating the working class, giving it a measure of decision-making power through collective bargaining and legal strikes: the recognition and institutionalization of the union movement. Economic equilibrium was to be accomplished by increasing demand to meet supply, through Fordism (the principle that workers should earn enough to buy the products made with their labor) and welfare (enabling even the unemployed to participate in the economy as buyers). In return for this universalization of the right to consume, the workers would agree to safeguard management profits by increasing their productivity apace with their wages. Capitalism with a human face: everybody happy, busily banking or consuming away (1997a, p. 7).

Here again, Marcuse and Habermas' influence is obvious—the individual's containment becomes a pleasant, self-sought prison, wallpapered with the illusion of meaningful participation. What seems like a naturally occurring reality is the product of ideological choices and the range of symbolic violences consequently set into play. Consider, for example, *The Truman Show* as a popular, contemporary representation of this process. In its depiction of a human life lived in a totally constructed and controlled reality this film addresses itself to questions of what constitutes reality and meaningful participation and who has the right to decide. In fact, this film indicates a growing awareness of the unravelling of many of the narratives of Fordist-Keynesian society. As part of this critique, there are any number of oblique references to the fashions and decor of the 1950s and 1960s, and the town/movie-set in which the story is set parallels the television shows of this era, down to the token appearance of a single black family. Like the nuclear family narrative, the reality-within-reality of Truman's life is constructed and normativized. An even more recent example of constructed reality is the emergence of 'reality' television. *Big Brother* grouped together a housebound group of young people and filmed them day and night as they responded to outside manipulations. Such a critique would have been unthinkable within the ideological climate of the years and the construction of the Fordist-Keynesian nationstate. The *Survivor* series is yet another example. High selective editing, carefully orchestrated events and total isolation are represented as 'reality' when in fact they are highly constructed and boundaried situations.

Accompanying and facilitating the economic and social transformation which characterized the immediate post-war years, was the dominance of the nationstate as the mediator of economic activity, and in fact, the rise to prominence of the nationstate can be viewed as one of the major de- and reterritorializations of capitalism in the modern era. Harvey (1990, p. 264) writes of this process of nation building and links it into contemporary shifts into globalization:

The vast expansion of foreign trade and investment after 1850 put the major capitalist powers on the path of globalism, but did so through imperial conquest and inter-imperialist rivalry that was to reach its apogee in World War 1—the first global war. En route, the world's spaces were deterritorialized, stripped of their preceding significations, and then reterritorialized according to the convenience of colonial and imperial administration.

The national borders of nations were instituted and legitimized during this period of territorial expansion by imperialist nationstates and redrawn yet again after the second global war of the late-1930s and early 1940s. The seeming naturalness and longevity of existing patterns of nationstates and the social narratives which accompanied them attests to the reach and persuasiveness of the symbolic violence which accompanied the Fordist-Keynesian era. Part and parcel of the solidification of nationstates was the linking of institutions, for example family and education, with their implicit assumptions of and requirement for, a particular idealized citizen, and economic trajectory. This interlocking system of social narratives and institutions constructed a seemingly self-evident reality.

FAMILY NARRATIVES

It is in this historical space that the Western idealization and theories of the oedipalized nuclear family rose to narrative status, where the narratives of the ideal citizen-worker and homemaker, and the Keynesian social contract become totally enmeshed. This represented yet another facet of the de-and reterritorializing flow of capitalism as women, subsumed within the male 'living' wage, became identified with the domestic space, and men and children were recreated within the spatio-temporal rhythms of industrial institutions—particularly school and workplace. These identities and social spatialities were legitimized within existing social theory and the emergent mass media encouraged us to conceive of ourselves in terms of social roles—of identities we could assume and inhabit. In this period, habitus formations were aggressively reshaped in the cross currents of economics and politics. A new society and a new social being was under construction.

In an age of mass media, television and print media held up living examples of the monocultural nuclear family in action for public consumption and reference: in Australia, generations of women have learnt what the perfect woman was and how to be one from magazines such as *Woman's Day, New Idea* and *The Australian Women's Weekly*. And this is not just an amusing Australian idiosyncrasy—versions of these magazines exist in every Western country. And, not just one magazine. These blueprints for womanhood dominated the magazine market, and their effect was reinforced and enhanced by other media forms, in particular, television.

Television shows delivered multi-modal tableaux of appropriate family forms, racial configurations and individual roles right into the living room. *Father Knows Best* reflected the narrative of the wise, patriarchal father/husband figure. Modelled here was the problem-solving and decision-making male role. This was extended to include family man-of-action in *Lost in Space*. Married women were always at home, draped around living room or kitchen scenery: remember the *Dick van Dyke Show, Bewitched* and *Lassie? The Patty Duke Show* and *Gidget* demonstrated appropriate female teenage roles and activities, while *Doby Gillis* and *My Three Sons* modelled the concerns and practices of 'normal' adolescent males. Pre-adolescent boys—not girls—were introduced to their roles as adventurers, risk-takers and decision-makers in programmes such as *Flipper, Lassie, Skippy* and *Gentle Ben*. Non-nuclear families were depicted. *My Three Sons,* for example, revolved around the daily lives of a widower and his sons. All referenced themselves against the 'perfect' nuclear family model and did the best they could in the circumstances. This is why they were loved by audiences around the world.

Missing from these shows were non-whites. Non-white men and women were either missing entirely or depicted in subservient, invisible domestic roles. Prime time television in the 1950s, 1960s and into the early 1970s was about white people, and they were living perfect nuclear lives in homogeneous, localized communities: a very strong message about happiness, health and success was being broadcast every day and night into millions of homes across the Western world. Simultaneously, mass education pivoted around the middle class, white nuclear family reflecting its gender roles, activities and spaces from the pages of every textbook. This era is memorable, in particular, for the advent of the generic, vocabulary-controlled instructional reading text—the basal reader. Looking out from the pages of these mass-produced and widely disseminated reading materials were a host of white, middle class nuclear families. The stories centered around the activities of white boys, with white girls looking on. Take, for example, series such as *Endeavour* and *Happy Venturers,* classics of the 1960s. In these stories, boys with names like 'Dick' play soccer, race the family dog, fly kites and protect their little sister from undertaking physical activity other than playing with dolls or the occasional shout of "Run Dick run". Nowhere in the mass produced reading texts of the 1950s and 60s are normal, everyday families depicted as anything other than white and comfortably middle class. Nowhere do mothers have a job, other than that of homemaker; nowhere are fathers unemployed; nowhere are these families non-white and/or non-nuclear.

CONCLUSION

In a period when the system of capitalism is demonstrably morphing we can expect the social conditions in which we live and in which we construct ourselves to also alter. Consequently, the framings through which we seek to impose order on our experiences will also alter. It is relevant, therefore, to trace the movement of capitalism away from the form which characterized the period from 1945 through to the early 1970s. The social structure which accompanied Fordist capitalism can be understood in relation to the complex entwining of the Keynesian social contract and its companion, Modernization Theory[23]. Fundamental to this particular understanding of the relationships between the state and its citizenry was the operation of certain key normative social narratives or, to borrow from Arieti

---

[23] Modernization theorists understood that modern values and practices—which would, they reasoned, end in economic development—could be grafted onto 'less developed' societies and nations via technology and the education of 'elites' (Leys 1996). This led to a series of technological and educational programmes. In the context of Cold War politics, it was also believed by some that modernization would ultimately lead to democracy. According to Leys (1996), there was a close connection between the principles of modernization theory and the aims of US foreign policy during this time.

(1967), 'paleosymbols'. Here, I am referring particularly to the set of relationships, practices and roles that have formed into the nuclear narrative. As capitalism as a system is indisputably changing rapidly, so too are the ways in which we must theorize its movements and impacts. As Braudel observes, "the worst error of all is to suppose that capitalism is simply an economic system" (1985, p. 623).

CHAPTER 6

CAPITALISM AFTER 1973

INTRODUCTION

The era following the Second World War saw the emergence of the United States as a hegemonic cultural, political and economic power, counterbalanced by the emergence of the Soviet bloc. The intersection of international politics, economic growth in the wake of the war and the ideological commitment to 'nation' led to the emergence of a set of key normative narratives—self, nuclear family, community and homogeneous nationstate. In other words, the Fordist nationstate. The early 1970s saw the beginning of an accelerating change in western capitalism. This Chapter begins to explore these changes and their implications for family.

AFTER 1973

The artificially created and maintained Keynesian equilibrium appeared to hold firm through the 1950s into the late 1960s and early 1970s. Throughout this period the nuclear narrative remained a primary normative mechanism. By this time, however, the social and economic climate was changing substantially as the post-war economic boom began to lose pace. In attempting to understand the shift out of Fordist capitalism, Harvey (1990) notes the intersection of a number of factors around the early 1970s, including the Arab-Israeli War, rising inflation in Western nations who found themselves with large amounts of excess investment dollars, and the OPEC decision to raise oil prices. The fallout from these collisions was felt throughout the remainder of the 1970s and into the 1980s, which Harvey characterizes as "a troubled period of economic restructuring and social and political readjustment" (p. 145). The needs of contemporary neoliberalism were planted during this era—Reagan's presidency in the United States and Thatcher's government in the United Kingdom laid the foundations of neoliberal strategy (McChesney 1999). For the West, this 'troubled period' seemed to suddenly appear with OPEC oil crises of the early 1970s and the sudden availability of large volumes of cash to previously marginal nations such as the Arab states. Suddenly the trading actions of one group of nations, even Third World nations, could impact on the daily lives of people in other parts of the world. While it is true that this has always been so, the oil crises of the 1970s brought this message into the living rooms and workplaces of every individual. The shock of this revelation was palpable. At this point, the Keynesian comfort zone began to unravel.

In this period the carefully constructed world order began to come loose around the edges. This is particularly evident from a consideration of the trajectory of the Third World and decolonizing nations during this time. In the immediate post-war-postcolonial era, newly independent nations—for example, Sukarno's Indonesia, Perón's Argentina, Tanzania, Ghana, Brazil, India and Egypt—had adopted either state-dominated autarkic or socialist strategies (Sachs 1998). Whichever approach was adopted, however, the effect was that these countries closed themselves off to open trading, adopting the position that they needed to be internally self-sufficient in order to become strong, unified nations. This approach was in line with the basic conceptual understandings which framed the Bretton-Woods agreements—that nationstates were autonomous and unified. We should note, however, that Third World nations were not entirely cut off from the global economic cycle. In practice, they were intricately linked via the economic loans of US-dominated World Bank and The International Monetary Fund (IMF) and the relationships of dependency which ensued (Leys 1996).

By the 1970s the process of decolonization which began immediately after the end of the war was almost complete and had two immediately identifiable outcomes. Firstly, colonial powers (Great Britain, France, Belgium, Portugal and the Netherlands) lost a steady source of income and guaranteed markets for their products, which inexorably reduced their access to large cash flows. Secondly, these newly independent nations, along with other Third World nations, became increasingly vocal in their demands for global political and economic reform, particularly given increasing suspicion regarding the role of the IMF and the World Bank in the maintenance of US economic hegemony (Sachs 1998)—the IMF and World Bank were established in the shadow of post-war American economic and political ascendancy. Significantly, the early 1980s heralded the beginning of a shift in Third World economic policy. In the 1980s many of these nations began to reconstruct their economic policies, adopting open trade strategies and entering the world trading and production scene. This was a significant turnaround in theory and practice. These reforms, some aimed at shifting the economic status quo, of necessity, chipped away at both the illusion and reality of US domination, particularly in light of the suspected complicity of the IMF and the World Bank in the maintenance of US economic hegemony in the Third World.

Reconceptualizing nationstate

The emergence of the Third World as a global political force coincided with the general collapse of Development Theory[24] (Leys 1996) and the optimism which had fuelled it. In 1973, the Bretton-Woods system of agreement was finally abandoned.

---

[24]   Key to Development Theory was the notion of economic development and growth. Sound economic theory and its implementation were, it was believed, crucial for the achievement of economic progress, particularly in Third World and newly decolonizing nations. Leys (1996) suggests that Development Theory was linked to the desire by colonial and ex-colonial powers to accelerate national economic growth.

Implicit in this major shift was the acknowledgment that nations were no longer capable of regulating currency flow or trade across their boundaries. At this moment, the nationstate was reconceptualized: no longer seen as the autonomous and central political unit in international affairs. The capitalist market had already moved to bypass trade and currency restrictions and the OPEC oil crises of the early 1970s were a clear and negative reminder of this. Once the homogeneous nationstate is no longer seen as the primary international unit, and this was the major admission of the end of Bretton-Woods, then the particular key narratives which were constructed to maintain its internal cohesion must, in time, lose their primacy.

In the vacuum created by the breakdown of currency regulation, international currency speculation took off, impacting significantly on commodity prices and currency values. By 1980, OECD (Organization for Economic Cooperation and Development) countries had abandoned domestic Keynesian economic policies (Leys 1996) recognizing that capital flows across and through national boundaries could no longer be regulated, and by the mid-1980s trade and capital were effectively deregulated throughout the world. In the aftermath of deregulation the General Agreement on Tariffs and Trade (GATT), the European Union's Single Market and Maastricht Treaties, and the North American Free Trade Agreement have codified contemporary principles of free trade across the globe.

The impact of decolonization on the processes of deregulation should not go unnoted. Decolonization was accompanied by internal social upheaval in numerous peripheral and semi-peripheral states: Iran, Nicaragua, El Salvador, the Philippines, Brazil, South Africa, South Korea, Poland and later all of Eastern Europe experienced social unrest (Reifer & Sudler 1996). This unrest continues in many areas. However, the erosion of imposed colonial identities saw an explosion of reclaimed, reformulated and newly emergent ethnic identifications, along with the theoretical articulation of this decoupling from colonialism in postcolonial theory (see, for example, the work of Amin 1976, 1977, 1990; Guha & Spivak 1988; Gunew 1994; Minh-ha 1989; Spivak 1990). This was a crucial moment in the history of the modern nationstate. Here it is important to discriminate between the ascribed identities which were imposed by outside powers during colonization and the self-acclaimed group identities which emerged as colonial influence receded. These new ethnicities were rallying points—subject positions outside colonialism and colonial domination. As such they continued to be highly politicized and constructed, formed around specific locales and/or political agendas. However, as in the space after the end of the Second World War, this was not a time of freedom to choose ethnic, racial or national identity: choice or assignation of identity was a political issue that continued to produce winners and losers. The lasting significance of the emergence of postcolonial nationalisms and identities lies in their problematization of existing patterns of 'nation'. Development Theory was itself premised upon particular understandings about national development, as I have already noted, and upon the primacy of the nationstate as an economic, political and cultural unit. The emergence of a postcolonial system of identifications was a final nail in the coffin of the ideologically unified Modernist nationstate and the international economic arrangements which were premised upon it.

Returning to the United States, the late 1970s and the early 1980s saw America lapse into economic decline, with rising interest rates and massively increasing national deficits[25]: during Ronald Reagan's presidency, the United States went from being the world's largest creditor nation to the largest debtor nation (Reifer & Sudler 1996). This was a significant turnaround, directly attributable to a shift in American policy toward remilitarization in response to the growing instability of the bipolar alignment and the resulting surge in localized conflicts. Contributing to this shift was the emergence of a new global trading market the United States no longer dominated or controlled: marking this decline, its share of world economic activity fell from two-thirds to one-half between 1960 and 1975 (Keohane 1989, cited in Clark 1997, p. 152).

The actions of the United States in this period could be described, then, as an attempt to regain a waning global hegemony in the face of the challenges posed by the Third World and the warming of the Cold War. This was clearly a world which still viewed itself in terms of autonomous nationstates, but facing increasing pressures sourced in the processes of globalization. It is fair to speculate that also implicit in this agenda was a perceived need to maintain the internal cohesion of the American nation after the destabilizing effects of the Vietnam conflict and civil rights movements of the 1960s and 70s. These intersecting currents of unrest, economic decline and a weakened global hegemony, mixed with the residual effects of positivist sciences and social theory encouraged the belief that a renewed military strength and the exercise of limited military action was a tenable solution. This led directly to escalating federal deficits throughout the Carter, Reagan and Bush presidencies and a deepening of US economic decline (Reifer & Sudler 1996). The rest of the Western world followed the United States into this slump. Australia, for instance, experienced large-scale unemployment and interest rates which peaked at over 17% in the mid-1980s, and, beginning in the late 1960s, OECD countries experienced a decline in average rates of growth—to around 2% (Leys 1996).

Market or 'neo' liberalism

In this new climate, governments have pursued "fiscal restraint, tax minimisation, deregulation and marketisation whether Republican or Democratic in the USA, Labor/Labour in Australia and Britain" (Marginson 1997, p. 57). Keynesian economic and social policies were abandoned and with them any real expectation of full employment. The new trend in government since the 1980s has been neoliberalism. From an Australian perspective, this era has been characterized by the concern of governments, at all levels, to facilitate a competitive economy and by a decreasing concern with and commitment to, social welfare (Marginson 1997).

---

[25]   In 1971, the United States experienced its first balance-of-payment since the turn of the century. As well, its gold reserves fell to $12.1 billion, less than half what they were in 1949 (Clark 1997).

Thus, neoliberalism encapsulates both a new economic and a new social project based around competition—both of markets and individuals. In Australia, market liberalism has been disseminated across political and economic systems: social welfare is increasingly specific and recipients are increasingly marginalized; universities have been restructured and directed to be self-regulating and partially self-funding (Marginson 1997); education is increasingly a 'user pays' system rather than a generally accessible right; private and public sector businesses have decentralized and devolved; and, the workers have had to come to terms with enterprise bargaining and the emergence of contract and part-time labor in lieu of the Keynesian social contract. In parallel with these changes, Australian federal governments[26] and large corporations[27] have aggressively integrated Australian industry and trade with that of other nations.

Returning to the international scene, the other major event to take place at this time was the reunification of Germany and the disintegration of the Soviet bloc, with the consequent decline of Soviet influence in the Third World. As with the decline of other colonial powers, the short term result of this move has been social unrest and localized conflict amongst former Soviet bloc countries. The world has watched the re-emergence of ethnic, racial and national identities and, in this volatile climate, unfortunate episodes of ethnic cleansing which continue to the present. Unfolding before the world media is the breakdown of what was once a comprehensive system of symbolic and overt violence and, in the aftermath, the conflict over a new order.

In relation to the argument of this Chapter the question arises as to how much this dismantling of the Eastern political and economic bloc is an outcome of the shifts in capitalism since the 1970s. Our immediate familiarity with the violence and despair in this series of conflicts is one aspect of the movement away from nationstate capitalism. Global technology makes these formerly unheard of places and people our neighbours. Their conflicts become ours and our experiences within globalizing capitalism have made it clear that the impact of these struggles is not necessarily limited to localized sites. That is, we do not see the world in terms of isolated nationstates and containable localized disputes, rather, within globalizing capitalism the connections within the global community are increasingly understood, and have been internalized into the habitus of the emerging citizen. It was in this climate of the obvious shift away from the primacy of the nationstate that Deleuze and Guattari (1983) formulated their notion of the capitalist axiomatic. They were referring to what they saw in the late 1960s and early 1970s as the increasing power of capitalism to reach into our everyday lives, to cross national boundaries or to recreate them. In the 1990s, the notion of the axiomatic becomes increasingly useful

---

[26] The reduction of tariffs and abolition of import quotas in the motor vehicle industry is an example of government-initiated restructuring in the Australian context. The connection of this industry with a global network has encouraged Australian car producers to export, but it has also meant that this sector is no longer a large and secure employer.

[27] Between 1980 and 1990, BHP refinanced, diversified and rationalized. In the process it 'shed' 12000 workers between 1982 and 1983, and transformed itself from a national company into an international corporation (Fagan & Webber 1994).

to describe the immanence and fluidity of capitalism. Also useful when attempting
to describe the fluidity and flux of capitalism is the notion of 'morphing'. In the
mid-1990s, Michael Jackson used morphing technology in a well-known video clip,
morphing with fascinating fluidity from one static shape to another. The film
Terminator II used the notion of morphing—the ability to change form, to become
fluid, to assume and then cast off a physical presence—to inject relentless
postmodern menace into its villain. Here, it is the lack of an original identity, and the
ensuing lack of history—the lack of empathy for a shape-bound enemy—that is truly
unsettling. Accentuating this unsettling is the potential for alternate and, as yet,
unimaginable realities glimpsed within this determined fluidity. Using this same
notion of morphing, the children's' television sci-fi series, *Animorphs,* taps into this
sense of unknown realities. There is no original or final form in this ongoing process
of de- and reterritorialization. Instead each momentary physical manifestation is
strategic and transitory. An appropriate and useful metaphor for conceptualizing
capitalism.

In its long history, capitalism has morphed its way through a number of
transformations, each more intrusive into the daily existence of individuals than the
last. There has always been an agenda of increasing globalization (Robertson 1992).
The identifiable shifts in the movement of capitalism since the end of World War
Two are cases in point. Immediately after the war, Fordist capitalism held sway and
social relations were constructed and maintained within a particular set of narratives
linked to the primacy of the modern nationstate. These narratives constitute
normative processes of symbolic violence. However the period after 1973 was one
of fundamental change: Bretton Woods and all that it symbolized in terms of the
primacy of the nationstate and the social relationships that accompanied it was
abandoned; the emergence of the Third World as an international player;
decolonization, and the destabilization this ultimately caused; the questioning of
identity that has followed the disruption to the nationstate narrative. For some, these
shifts are markers of the emergence of a substantively different society (see, for
example, Castells 1997, 1997, 1998; Lee 1996); for others, these shifts are not
unexpected within the imperatives of the capitalist flow (Deleuze and Guattari 1987;
Guattari 1985; Massumi 1992, 1997b). Regardless, commentators share the
observation that capitalism has undergone substantial evolution in a relatively brief
time period. For many, the term 'globalization' is used to describe the qualitatively
different form of capitalism which has emerged over the last fifteen years.
Globalizing capitalism defies strict delineation in the Modernist sense—it is more
useful to imagine it in terms of the strategic and transitory territorializations of
morphing or as an ongoing 'flow'.

THE INFORMATION SOCIETY—FAST, LATE, GLOBALIZING CAPITALISM

What do we mean when we talk about 'globalization' and 'globalizing capitalism'?
Theorists such as Deleuze and Guattari would not, I suspect, be surprised by the turn
towards globalization. From their perspective, capitalism is being true to its nature,

becoming increasingly pervasive and controlling. And, although Wilden would applaud the sudden visibility of the state-nation overlay, he would be keen to identify the processes of symbolic violence which will underwrite new ideological patterns.

What sets the current era apart is the speed and impact of technology and the consequent scope of the changes wrought by capitalism to impact on the lives of every individual. The emergence of new communications technologies has made possible the immanence of globalizing capitalism. Many commentators identify the new information technologies as the defining characteristic of this era, setting it apart from all others (Castells 1996, 1997, 1998; Harvey 1990; Webster 1995). Included amongst these is Manuel Castells, whose central argument is that:

> the development of IT networks around the globe promotes the importance of information flows for economic and social organization while simultaneously it reduces the significance of particular places. It follows that, in the 'informational economy', a major concern of organizations becomes the management of and response to information flows. This is in keeping with the geographer's concern with spatial relationships, a central argument being that information networks and the consequent circulation of information results in organisations becoming increasingly able to transcend limitations formerly imposed by place (Webster 1995, p. 199).

Webster goes on to note that information networks have been implicated in both the centralization and decentralization of economic and social organization. These two processes, in fact, go on concurrently. The rapid expansion of technology and information have created an economy where information is the product around which the market pivots.

For many commentators there is the feeling that capitalism has taken flight, that it has moved to a new plane of existence away from the material, place-bound production of an earlier era towards the ephemeral world of finance capital and the information economy. I quote Harvey in this regard:

> The new financial systems put into place since 1972 have changed the balance of forces at work in global capitalism, giving much more autonomy to the banking and financial system relative to corporate, state, and personal financing. Flexible accumulation evidently looks more to finance capital as its co-ordinating power than did Fordism. This means that the potentiality for the formation of independent and autonomous monetary and financial crises is much greater than before, even though the financial system is better able to spread risks over a broader front and shift funds rapidly from failing to profitable enterprises, regions, and sectors. Much of the flux, instability, and gyrating can be directly attributed to this enhanced capacity to switch capital flows around in ways that seem almost oblivious of the constraints of time and space that normally pin down material activities of production and consumption (1990, p. 164).

Harvey's text contains a hint of crisis. Yet as Massumi (1997b) argues, these crises have been subsumed within the total process of capitalism. Crisis is now normal: the flux and instability, the ephemerality Harvey notes, marks the internalization by capitalism of existing constraints and its subsequent evolution. This was precisely Habermas' point. The engulfing of crisis by capitalism was noted by Habermas (1973, 1979) in the early 1970s. While capitalism tends, by its movement, to create crises of various forms, these are disseminated over a wide section of the social order—as Habermas notes, crises can be "administratively processed and transferred, by stages, through the political and into the socio-cultural system" (1973, p. 40) creating a state of permanent mobilization (Marcuse 1956). Habermas understood clearly that crisis was normal—the normalized and normalizing state of mass capitalism. In fact, serial crises have become essential to the dynamic movement of capitalism and a part of the normative machinery of a capitalist social order. They are yet another way of controlling the activities of individuals and groups.

Deleuze and Guattari would understand this movement of capitalism as a deterritorialized and deterritorializing flow which is following its natural tendency for flux and instability (1983, 1987). The changes which are evident in the shift away from the dominance of Fordist narratives of capitalism towards globalization and fast capitalism can be seen as the fluidity of this deterritorializing flow and the nature of life itself. Capitalism deterritorializes and then reterritorializes as the direction of its self-created crises require. Thus, where some continue to read crisis into the recent morphing of capitalism, a Deleuzian understanding tells us that these are part and parcel of this system.

Core understandings

The process of globalization is generally associated with an increase in the density and depth of economic interdependencies and international interactions (Clark 1997; Eden & Potter 1993; Held 1995; Wallace 1995;); information technology (Castells 1996, 1998; Harvey 1990) and increasing social interdependence (Castells 1997; Friedman 1995; Robertson 1992). Additionally there is also a connection to the proliferation of nongovernmental and international organizations such as the United Nations and Greenpeace (Clark 1997). Clearly, theorists from a number of perspectives have noted shifts in capitalism, however many experience a difficulty in conceptualizing the encompassing nature of this shift. Beginning to weave these threads together into a coherent picture of what is taking place, Albrow (1997) draws upon the works of a number of globalization theorists to construct a set of three core propositions about globalization. The first is 'globalism' where increasingly, the ways in which individuals and groups understand their world is in global terms. No longer are we confined to localized and space-bound communities. The rapid expansion of technological capacity has impacted on the ways in which we experience the world.

The second of these currents, 'globality', focuses on the increasing worldwide availability and impact of "images, information and commodities" (Albrow 1997, p. 44). And finally, drawing from the work of Harvey (1990), Albrow describes the importance of time-space compression in contemporary globalization. Information, commodities and people now move with formerly unimaginable speed around the globe, changing the meaning of time and distance. These currents, technological and social, are resulting in an increasing *disembeddedness*, whereby persons are able to maintain satisfactory social and financial contact with relatives, business associates and cultural practices wherever they are located. In a globalizing world, community is no longer place-bound and this has vast implications for identity and nation. Harvey (1990) also attempts to analyze gobalization. He pinpoints two pivotal developments which characterize this new capitalism. First, the capitalism which has emerged from this time of readjustment has picked up pace in many respects, and this is where the attention of many has turned to the so-called 'information society' (Castells 1996; Webster 1995) and the notion of advanced or fast capitalism. Second, there has emerged out of all of this a complexly coordinated global financial system. As Harvey describes the process:

> the formation of a global stock market, of global commodity (even debt) futures markets, or currency and interest rate swaps, together with an accelerated geographical mobility of funds, meant, for the first time, the formation of a single world market for money and credit supply (1990, p. 161).

Contemporary commentators have begun to use the term 'new economies' to indicate these new characteristics. For Harvey, the current shift into a global financial circuit, to new economies, has had a two-pronged effect:

> ...on the one hand towards the formation of financial conglomerates and brokers of extraordinary global power, and, on the other hand, a rapid proliferation and decentralization of financial activities and flows through the creation of entirely new financial instruments and markets (1990, pp. 160-161).

Sinuous, malleable and astoundingly responsive to any and all fluctuations, capitalism has repeatedly morphed in response to sea changes in the social and the economic, new modes of production and the opening of new technological vistas. It has become the axiomatic flow predicted by Deleuze and Guattari.

Missing from many explanatory frameworks of globalizing capitalism are the implications for people's everyday lives, for changing constructions of the ideal citizen-worker, of family, of identity. Purely economic (Sachs 1998; Wallerstein 1991), political (Clark 1997), and technological (Harvey 1990; Webster 1995) analyses of these changes in capitalism are unable to adequately incorporate sociocultural impact. Rattansi (1994, p. 27) observes that:

> Globalization means, among other things, that the cultural boundaries of nation-states are breached in myriad ways, creating opportunities for cultural cosmopolitanisms of various kinds, but also generating anxieties which are experienced in different ways by locales and their populations, and managed and mobilized through a range of strategies by local and national state agencies, political parties.

The construction of a core set of understandings about what is taking place within contemporary capitalism should in no way lead us to expect that globalization is a homogeneous, linear process. Far from it. Instead, the term 'globalization' has become the marker of a complex set of contradictory and shifting processes. Albrow's three key propositions—globalism, globality and time-space compression—are not however clearly defined categories of experience. Those of us who live privileged middle class lives often experience these propositions as positives. We have the resources (economic, cultural and social) to travel for work and pleasure; we have internet access and international managed share portfolios, increasing wage levels and heightened life expectations. For many others, contemporary globalization has delivered declining standards of living as well as increasingly limited hope for upward social mobility. Many experience mobility as *immobility*—with a heightened local impact on life chances and trajectories. Location has emerged as a key indicator of life chances in new economies (Edgar 1999). Time-space compression is experienced as the withdrawal of employment opportunities and erosion of community resources. Thus, the process of globalization is profoundly uneven and its outcomes in various sites often take the form of resistance and resentment politics, pluralism and the rise of non-state nationalisms. Fagan and Webber (1994) argue that:

> the social impacts of global change have been sharply *uneven* as industrialized societies have become more socially and spatially polarised since the end of the long boom. People's experience of economic change is affected increasingly by things like their gender, age, social class, and place (p. 29).

Yet, it is not just economic change that is mediated by the specific positioning of persons. So too social and cultural change; so too material change. Regardless of how we generalize the actual processes of globalization, their uptake by people is *always* mediated by localized conditions. There can be no discussion of globalization without also of fragmentation and heterogeneity. They are aspects of the same process. We must move beyond a positioning of fragmentation and homogeneity as polemic oppositions which are an outcome of the shift to globalizing capitalism.

As with postmodernism, there is no strict delineation and much confusion regarding the concept of globalization. We must be careful to avoid the presumption that globalization is a strictly recent phenomenon and that it is homogeneous. Beginning to address confusion around this term, Peiterse (1995) notes that there are as many notions of globalization as there are social sciences, and goes on to describe them:

> In economics, globalization refers to economic internationalization and the spread of capitalist market relations...In international relations, the focus is on the increasing density of interstate relations and the development of world politics. In sociology the concern is with increasing world-wide social densities and the emergence of 'world society'. In cultural studies, the focus is on global communications and world-wide cultural standardization, as in CocaColonization and McDonaldization, and on postcolonial culture. In history, the concern is with conceptualizing 'global history' (p. 45).

Here, Peitserse focuses on the breadth of the impact of globalization. Numerous disciplines are using this term to describe specific patterns of change which have emerged quite recently. Each of them is describing one subset of the larger process of globalization as a sociological phenomenon. This broader understanding shares with Deleuze and Guattari's axiomatic the belief that capitalism is more than an economic or political system. It constitutes the material and social processes which characterize the current period.

An additional point needs to be made here. This recent, rapid escalation across a number of zones of activity should not encourage us to believe that globalization, as a process, has appeared suddenly. Far from it. While the focus here is the impact of globalization in contemporary terms, this ongoing process has a long history that can be traced back to the rise of world religions. Robertson writes:

> As a form with its own dynamics it began to take shape during the period of the decline of feudalism in Europe. During that period there was an acceleration in the early shaping of the nationally organized society; the mounting thematization of the (primarily male) individual; the enhancement of the system of inter-state relations; and the beginnings of modern ideas of humanity, particularly in philosophy and in early international law (1992, p. 182).

What Robertson is in fact indicating is that the history of capitalism has been the history of globalization. Deleuze and Guattari's vision of the axiomatic sits well with this account. The current phase is an acceleration of this process and we have begun to use the term 'globalization' in order to foreground the characteristics peculiar to this acceleration. But what of the nationstate within this shift? How does globalization impact upon the nationstate?

Globalization and nationstate

Drawing specifically from international relations, Clark (1997) makes a direct link between the end of the Cold War and the acceleration of globalization. Sachs (1998) identifies this same era as a time of fundamental policy change across the nations of the developing world—away from State controlled closed trading systems to open systems. Of course, these two observations are not unrelated. Clark writes of the absence of an international security agenda in the wake of the Cold War collapse that has allowed capitalism, unchecked, to shape itself (1997, p. 183). The principles of normativity that were established and maintained within Modernist epistemology were linked to the requirements and effects of the modern nationstate, and beyond that, to existing patterns of global security. The cultural and social spaces of the nationstate were constructed in relation to these security agendas, and there are demonstrable links between the narrative of the nuclear family, the notion of a unified 'self', and the state. It is within this discourse that ethnicity and race have been used as markers of inclusion or exclusion, depending on the relative advantage offered to the economic and security agendas of each state. Of course, any number of ethnic and/or racial identifications predate the modern nationstate. However, the nationstate has co-opted these classificatory systems for its own interests and incorporated them into the normative discourses that create and police the sociocultural space of the nation.

Changing landscapes of nation

The trajectory of the modern nationstate can be traced to the seventeenth century (Hirst & Thompson 1996) and is philosophically linked to the trajectory of 'reason' as a legacy of the French Revolution (Touraine 1990). Central to recognition of 'nation' was acknowledgment that "each state was the sole political authority with exclusive possession of a defined territory" (Hirst & Thompson 1996, p. 171). The French Revolution, then, is associated with "creating and defending the unity of the nation, identified with the universal principles of reason, liberty and equality, against all its internal and external enemies" (Touraine 1990, p. 124). Modern capitalism has also been traced to this historical period (Robertson 1992), hence the well-known connection between rationality, the modern nationstate and industrial capitalism. The connection between the notion of the integrated rational 'self', community and nationstate is clear, as is the drive for internal control and homogeneity. The nationstate of modern Western history was ideologically homogenous—constructed and, as they became increasingly committed to peaceful control of citizens, maintained by normative narratives such as the nuclear family, sanity and democracy.

In the shift out of Keynesian social and economic policies and in the face of increasing globalization, the role and salience of the nationstate has come under scrutiny. States no longer have guaranteed autonomy—either in terms of economic issues or ability to maintain internal homogeneity. There has been a distinct decoupling of 'nation' (the overlay of physical site, people and their belief in a unified group identity) and 'state' (the government). The concept of 'nation' is fragmenting into diverse ethnic and other allegiances while the State seems to represent an increasingly smaller segment of the population. While the State continues, its relationship to a unified national identity with which to mobilize the populace is problematic. However, according to Hirst and Thompson (1996), nationstates maintain a position of centrality in a globalizing world:

> Nation states are now simply one class of powers and political agencies in a complex system of power from world to local levels, but they have a centrality because of their relationships to territory and population. Populations remain territorial and subject to the citizenship of a national state (p. 190).

A shift has taken place in the function and field of interest of late capitalist nationstates, however their ongoing complicity in the processes of globalization has never been questioned. In terms of the nationstate, globalization can be understood, then, as a "pluralization of organizational forms" (Pieterse 1995, p. 53), rather than as indicative of decline. Modern globalization has not sounded the death knell of the nationstate. It is clear is that the nationstate is not about to disappear from the international scene, although some would argue that its power has been drastically curtailed (see, for example, Luke 1995). There are some who take up these changes to argue that the modern nationstate was an historical construct—"at best, an unstable historical construct aimed at containing the political, geographical and cultural landscape of Modernist Europe"—whose time has passed (Luke 1995, p. 94). For Luke, then, the nationstate has been effectively subsumed within global interdependencies. This critique highlights a salient issue: just as the nuclear family is an idealized and normative narrative, so too, the nationstate exists fundamentally as an idealized narrative, linked to the agendas of the Modernist theoretical and cultural project. By this account, nationstate becomes the idealized context of an idealized self and family formation, each in their own way constituting the normative principles of a specific historical epoch.

It has been, and seems set to remain, a key player. However, as Appadurai (1990) suggests, its role is not as clear cut and autonomous as it was within a Fordist-Keynesian regime. Appadurai alludes to the increasingly complex role played by the state within globalizing capitalism:

> The globalization of culture is not the same as its homogenization, but globalization involves the use of a variety of instruments of homogenization (armaments, advertising techniques, language hegemonies, clothing styles and the like), which are absorbed into local political and cultural economies, only to be repatriated as heterogeneous dialogues of national sovereignty, free enterprise, fundamentalism, etc., in which the state plays an increasingly delicate role: too much openness to global flows and the nation-state is threatened with revolt...; too little, and the state exits the international stage...(1990).

Rather than being sidelined, the state is thoroughly implicated in this process and continues to be a key player in the process of globalizing capitalism, engaging according to its own agendas. Modern nationstates have created and encouraged the enabling conditions for the emergence of globalizing capitalism.   Since the seventeenth century, globalization has gathered momentum with the complicity of nationstates. For many of these nationstates, it has been to their advantage to accommodate, if not encourage the processes now generically known as globalization. The state, then, is a major stakeholder in the politics of globalization (see, for example, Fagan & Webber 1994). Rather than disappearing, the nationstate is in the process of reconfiguring itself spatially. At present, this spatial reconfiguration refers more to the sociocultural and racial space of the nation rather than to physical territory. As security and economic activities have altered in the wake of the end of the Cold War and the decline of US hegemony, the need for a particular type of citizen, a particular type of family unit and a particular ethnic/racial shaping of the citizenry has also altered. The principles of normativity which formerly acted to maintain the sociocultural space of the nation (and which were linked directly to the security and economic agendas of each state) have ceased to be as vital as they once were. The contemporary Australian experience can be illuminating on this point.

As outlined earlier, the current Australian federal government has aggressively attempted to reconstruct 'traditional' family. This programme has taken a number of subtle pathways including the creation of an economic climate which 'encourages' women in lower paid jobs to 'choose' to reassume the homemaker-wife-mother role. This social reconstruction is accompanied by cutbacks in aged care, benefits for the young unemployed and students and child care allowances. Women, in particular, are targeted via calls for a reconstitution of traditional family. Withdrawal from welfare responsibility, both in moral and dollar terms, represents one outcome of the dismantling of Keynesian policy. The decision to reinvent the family is not the sole avenue to this policy target; rather, it is a patently ideological choice. But, the really interesting aspect is the heated debate that has risen around this issue. Predicting a female-voter backlash, one respondent noted:

> Most women work, want to work and are proud to work. They may yearn for more
> flexible hours or more family friendly employment. But what they want from a prime
> minister is someone who understands the pressures of their lives, not one who seeks to
> return them to the world of the cookie recipe, the frilly apron and the coffee morning
> (Sieghart 1998, p. 13).

Comments such as these reflect the irreversible changes that have taken place since
the 1960s in the workplace and in western societies generally. Sieghart refers
specifically to the experiences of women, arguing that those currently under forty-
five are "not likely suddenly to start believing that wives should be subservient or
that men should get the best jobs" as they grow older (p. 13). Women are
increasingly well educated—this is unlikely to change. As well, more women
around the world have greater control of their reproduction—this is also unlikely to
change. These mark significant, and I believe, irreversible changes for women since
the nuclear vision of the 1950s and 1960s. The experiences of men and children
have also altered markedly in the shift out of Fordist economies into globalizing
capitalism: just as women have challenged gender stereotypes, so too have men
begun to problematize and reconfigure expectations of masculinity (Connell 1995,
1997; Mills 1997). Women's Network Australia, The Older Women's Network and
the Young Women's Christian Association have all argued against the Howard
Government's attempts at re-naturalizing the place of women in the home, noting
that the financial incentives aimed at allowing women to stay at home are an attempt
at marginalizing women and shaping a "new Australian society in which the father
goes to work and the mother stays home with the children—a return to the 1950s"
(Olsson 1998, p. 26).

The strength of the response to this agenda indicates that the nuclear family is no
longer universally accepted by the middle classes as the necessary cornerstone of the
social order. The resistance with which conservative attempts to remake the
traditional family have been met suggest that the normative value of this narrative
has been destabilized; that the myth is losing its pedagogic power. It is my sense of
the matter that some sections of Western society feel somehow unsettled, in flux,
changing, and without direction. I suggest that this is because the prevailing
normative principles of the modernist nationstate are given decreasing legitimation
as the need for them decreases in the late twentieth century, but at the same time no
new narratives have emerged which so thoroughly link individual with family with
state.

Debt and symbolic violence

What *has* emerged is a new relationship with debt. As we have seen, the
fundamental shift from nationstate to globalizing capitalism has been characterized
by changes in the relative value and fluidity of capital. That is, in advanced
capitalism, capital has been cut loose from production—value is determined by
differential access to credit rather than by productive capacity or solid assets. This
represents a fundamental shift away from the Fordist production-consumption cycle.
This shift has, I believe, been made possible by the expansion of debt—the

emergence of a fast capitalist debtor culture. Usefully, Harvey (1990) has brought up the pivotal role of debt in advanced capitalism and linked it to desire. While the oedipalized narrative of family required the repression of desire, in economic terms, this translated to a delay in gratification. In this view, a once-only exchange between currency and goods was appropriate—the worker worked, was paid, saved, waited, and then exchanged these savings for consumer goods. However, fast capitalism increasingly requires the "debt-financing of present gratifications as one of its principal engines of economic growth" (Harvey 1990, p. 202). Here, there has been a substantial shift away from once-only exchanges to ongoing debt. Increasingly, the moral requirement for delayed gratification in relation to consumer goods is eroding. The point is that 'capital' is no longer indicative of money per se. Capital has flowed beyond this limit, and is now a signifier of value, a marker of desire rather than a standardized measure of direct exchange. In concert, desire refuses to be associated solely with the familial relationship and the development of normal sexuality and identity. In Bourdieuian terms, there has been a field shift accompanied, perhaps driven, by a reshuffling of the differential value applied to various capitals. Where nationstate capitalism created fields which recognized the superior social value of convertible currency, the shift to globalizing capitalism has redeployed the assignation of value—a shift in the means and mode of exchange. The effect of this is heightened when we note that capital can now decode and evolve faster than it can be recaptured by social processes.

There is an interesting link to be made here between changes in the construction of desire in changing economic times and the notions of discipline and control. The view of debt as a measure of individual and/or societal dysfunction or as evidence of blatant mismanagement which has characterized economic debates for any number of years is a marker of oedipalized closed system thinking and characterizes what Deleuze (1997, p. 310) terms "disciplinary societies". Deleuze notes that in "disciplinary societies one was always starting again (from school to the barracks, from the barracks to the factory) while in societies of control one is never finished with anything..." (p. 310). Disciplinary social formations are premised upon the experience of serial "apparent acquittal" while societies which are premised upon control are characterized by "limitless postponements" (p. 310), or in other words, debt.

In the shift from Fordist to beyond-Fordist economies we have experienced a drift from disciplinary society to society of control, with the disciplinary institutions now playing roles in a complex weave of ongoing controls. We are experiencing a change in the processes of symbolic violence. The shift in the consumption cycle which has taken place in the movement from a disciplinary to controlling society can be readily seen and experienced. Consider for example, special events: there has been a drift from emphasis on discrete, *very* special events (e.g. birthdays, Christmas) for which we were encouraged to save and wait, to aggressive marketing of a virtually overlapping series of newly-emphasised or created special events (birthday, anniversary, Mother's Day, Father's Day, Easter, Christmas, End of Financial Year Sale, New Year Sale, Back to School Sale). These events represent a shift from the *discipline* of delayed gratification to the ongoing *control* of serial gratification. While many of the holidays celebrated in the West are historical artefacts linked to other modes of production, they have been appropriated into the service of this emergent form of capitalism. Pivotal to the new emphasis on serial gratification is the emerging new relationship between the individual and debt.

Capital, thus, has morphed away from a reliance on physical, grounded wealth and the discipline of accumulating only what you can afford now (which served to link the individual directly into the Fordist production cycle), shifting to the control invoked via debt and the gratification of serial desire: "Man (sic) is no longer man enclosed, but man in debt" (Deleuze 1997, p. 312). The present operation of capitalist markets has moved to a pervasive and invasive 'control' which Deleuze describes as "short-term...rapid...continuous and without limit" (p. 312). Thus, capital becomes a mode of desire rather than a closed system of financial investment fixed to production. However, its connection to personal debt accumulation constitutes an ongoing control. The use of personal credit cards illustrates this shift. In contemporary America, only around thirty per cent of credit card users pay back their debt in full each month (Ritzer 1998). This means that around seventy per cent of all American credit card users practice serial, never-ending debt. These patterns of credit card usage are an example of the shift from discrete debt events to serial debt—from overt discipline to ongoing control and a new configuration of symbolic violence as we reorient to personal debt.

Conclusion

This is a necessarily broad picture description of global shifts in the capitalist flow. The post-war world realigned itself around Cold War economic and political blocs. The Fordist economic system, Modernization Theory, positivist sciences were, along with the nuclear narrative, mutually reinforcing and regulatory. However, the relatively rapid shift from nationstate capitalism to globalization has problematized these formerly self-evident 'truths'. Since the 1970s, then, we have seen that the process of globalization has multiple sources and a multiplicity of ostensibly contradictory consequences. Rather than the overwhelming homogeneity which accompanies the concept of an axiomatic, we are faced at the beginning of the twenty-first century with increasing heterogeneity as the global is taken up in the local spaces of individual lives.

Part Two has outlined the key transformations in our economic system. What of the social and cultural structures that are interlinked with the economic? Part Three takes up this question.

PART THREE

NEW TIMES: NEW FAMILIES

...it's (the family) continued existence probably signifies a good deal less than is hoped for....The family can only be preserved as a neutralized 'cultural institution' and such a preservation threatens its very life

(The Frankfurt School, 1972, p. 139).

CHAPTER 7

ETHNICITY AND RACE TO INTERETHNICITY

INTRODUCTION

There has been a lot going on since the close of World War Two hostilities. In the second half of this century, capitalism has transformed itself from Fordist-Keynesian production and society—strongly dependent upon territorial claims established via imperialist activities—towards increasing globalization, the permeability of nationstate boundaries and a new emphasis on institutional and individual performativity. The emergence of transnational corporations has facilitated this movement into capitalist globalization. This, and the enabling weakening of Fordism, has problematized and reframed the role of the nationstate. Capitalism's reach can now be discussed in global terms and increasingly, as a significant contributor to the minute and private details of the lives of individuals. As well, the changing hegemonic balance of the global econopolitical sphere has meant that there is an increasing trend towards (re)formulating and reclaiming ethnic identifications. Where it was once considered self-evident that race and culture were markers of innate difference, this notion is increasingly problematized in postmodern and postcolonial theory. The new emphasis in philosophic poststructuralism on the existence of multiple subjectivities has meant that the new ethnic and racial identifications individuals and groups may assume are no longer taken to be essential characteristics. It is here that this Chapter begins.

Race and culture

According to Ashcroft, Griffith and Tiffin (1998, p. 198), "the notion of race assumes, firstly, that humanity is divided into unchanging natural types, recognizable by physical features that are transmitted 'through the blood' and permit distinctions to be made between 'pure' and 'mixed' races". This is an interesting distinction in an historical moment where relative numbers of interracial and intercultural marriages are rapidly increasing (Price 1993a, 1996).

Race, as a definitive category, is linked strongly to the constructed dualism between primitive (traditional) and civilized (modern) societies which has characterized modern European social theory and structural anthropology. Underpinning the use of race as a classificatory system is a commitment to hierarchical social arrangements, linked to strategies of, and for, dominance (Ashcroft et al. 1998). Historically, these patterns of dominance have been constructed by, and to the advantage of, white colonial nations and the power elites that have directed key policy. Luke and Luke (1998, p. 729) describe these classificatory systems and the institutions structured around them as "early twentieth-century technologies of surveillance". They go on to argue that "identifications of skin colour and phenotypical features are typically equated in the public imaginary as part of a 'readable' code of difference, ranging from lack and defect to exoticism and 'noble savage' primitivism (1998, p. 731). Thus, race, as a modern category, emerged as a corollary of Western colonialism and its attempt to construct a pro-Western hierarchy which justified its political and mercantile aggression. Fordist societies maintained race as a substantive marker of difference, but as the civil rights movement of the 1960s demonstrated this was highly emotive and contested. Increasing racial hybridity has further problematized the notion of race as a clearly delineated system for categorizing people.

Race has been and will continue to be a marker of genetic heritage and will continue to invoke particular 'readings'. However, in the current destabilization of nationstate narratives increasing numbers of individuals are foregrounding other aspects of identity. Ethnicity is amongst these. The use of race as a classifier, in the older sense, is fading in the shift to new times. Intermarriage and racial blending, along with shifts in the global political and economic context, are blurring and boundaries and problematizing the practicalities of strictly delineated and hierarchical colour-coding systems. While contemporary racisms exist, they are increasingly a response to the instability and rapid change experienced within globalizing capitalism (see, for example, Stratton 1998). This has been seen in Australia in the late 1990s to the present as issues around immigration have been used as rallying points for far-right politics. As I write, the Australian government is in the throes of an international crisis as it refuses to allow more than 400 refugees from Afghanistan to land on Australian territory. As a result these people, including pregnant women and children, are languishing on the deck of the Norwegian tanker that rescued them from their sinking boat. Armed force is being used to ensure containment on the tanker. It has become an issue of international concern with no immediate end in sight, other than the tarnishing of Australia's humanitarian record and standing in the world community. This very troubling crisis follows on the heels of a series of events and debates relating to the forced detention and subsequent treatment of illegal immigrants, the vast majority of whom are from non-white nations. The issue of race and nation lies very close to the surface in these matters. Australia has historically struggled with a vocabulary for discussing race and as a result, this episode was framed in terms of enforcement of national boundaries. Being seen to have the ability to control one's physical borders has new meaning in a globalizing world particularly for an unpopular government in the midst of an election campaign. However, these unfortunate events notwithstanding, along with ethnicity, race is increasingly a positive identification—adopted and used by groups and by individuals to their own advantage, rather than experienced as exclusionary devices. These identifications become, in this scenario, strategic moves in a fast-paced and changeable game.

Ethnicity

Ethnicity is, according to Ashcroft, Griffiths and Tiffin (1998, p. 80), "a powerful identifier because while he or she chooses to remain in it, it is an identifier that cannot be denied, rejected or taken away by others". This has, until recently, been the crucial difference between race and ethnicity. Where race has been employed as an instrument of domination over various individuals and groups, ethnicity has more often been a self-chosen identifier. Hence, while race has been imposed on various groups according to genetic and physical attributes of difference, ethnicity "is usually deployed as an expression of positive self-perception" (Ashcroft et al. 1998, p. 80). This does not mean that ethnic identifications have not been used to create and maintain patterns of domination and subordination. They have. The experiences of European Jews and gypsies, the Irish-British conflict, and ongoing ethnic cleansing and conflict in former Soviet nations, are cases in point. These are disputes amongst ethnic, rather than racial, groups in struggles to achieve political agendas. Thus, the flip-side of these political struggles remains the attempt to construct particular racial and/or ethnic characteristics as negative markers of difference and deficit. These two agendas are travelling companions, their importance heightened by the tensions between the global and the local which characterize the globalization of capitalism. It is here, in this coexistence, that ethnicity and other imagined communities become increasingly influential social constructions.

What we are seeing, in the emergence of these new ethnic and racial identifications is a "new cultural politics which engages rather than suppresses difference and which depends, in part, on the cultural construction of new ethnic identities" (Hall 1996, p. 446). In the newly emergent configurations of globalized capitalism, ethnicity and race as definitive categories in the modernist sense are increasingly problematized (Featherstone 1991; Nash 1989; Omi & Winant 1986; Rattansi 1994; Rex 1986). As Hall notes, the new politics of representation, of which ethnicity and race are part, is a "process of unsettling, recombination, hybridization and 'cut-and-mix'" (1996, p. 447). Race remains a crucial identifier, nevertheless. However, as a strategic and positive identification, race, is increasingly taking on ethnicity's potential for empowerment—made possible by the destabilization of the nationstate and the emerging politics of difference.

As Harvey (1990, 1996), Castells (1998) and Robertson (1992) tell us, globalization is a contradictory and uneven process resulting in intensified localizations. Thus, while arbitrary boundaries are on one hand shifting there is, on the other hand, increasing pressure to form localized identities and allegiances. This reflects what can be understood as the push-pull effect of globalization (Luke & Carrington in press) where the impact of the global on the local and the local on the global create Robertson's (1995) 'glocalization'. In today's neoliberal marketplace an ethnic identification is only one of multiple, shifting and often contradictory subjectivities which any one individual may adopt according to context (Featherstone 1990; Giddens 1991; Jackson 1993). New and reclaimed ethnicities, many of which cut across racial categories, reflect these contradictory processes. Ethnicity, as a facet of groups and individual identity, must be understood as strategic and thusly linked directly to changing 'readings' of social, economic and political currents.

Drawing from Cornel West, Hall (1996) identifies three general characteristics of contemporary life: the displacement of European high culture, representing a shift in definitions of culture; cultural globalization; and, a fascination with difference. Ethnic difference, in particular, has caught the contemporary imagination, and while European high culture and modernity in general had a very limited vocabulary with which to deal with ethnicity and increasingly hybridized racial mixes, global postmodernism is drawn to difference (Hall 1996). Suddenly, Japanese anime is very trendy and popular in Australia and The United States—animated series, action figurines, fashion and printed text are all visibly influenced by this cultural form. Calvin Klein models are increasingly Eurasian and big budget Hollywood movies can be produced on the crowd-pulling ability of Asian actors such as Jet Li and Jackie Chan. Foreign language films, for example *Crouching Tiger, Hidden* Dragon, are now serious contenders at the Academic Awards, a sure sign of mainstream approval. There are many other examples of the value-addedness of 'difference'. This new politics of difference is, however, inherently contradictory and floating, mirroring the processes of globalization. Ethnic and racial conflict are still our constant companion: in Australia last week, a group of Lebanese boys were convicted of the apparently race related gang rape of two Anglo-Australian girls; Britain is wracked by race riots as systemically unemployed young men living in poorly serviced housing estates become increasingly alienated; and the world watches a new generation experience ethnic and religious conflict as 4 and 5 year old Catholic school girls in Ireland, escorted by armed riot police, walk the gauntlet of venomous abuse and violence hurled at them by Protestants as they are taken to school via a 'Protestant' street. Trying to capture in text this process of cultural shift and the emergence of marginality as a legitimate cultural position, Hall writes:

> Within culture, marginality, though it remains peripheral to the broader mainstream, has never been such a productive space as it is now. And that is not simply the opening within the dominant of spaces that those outside it can occupy. It is also the result of the cultural politics of difference, of the struggles around difference, of the production of new identities, of the appearance of new subjects on the political and cultural stage. This is true not only in regard to race but also for other marginalized ethnicities...(p. 467).

While Touraine (1995) has attempted to address changes in the exclusionary tendencies of advanced capitalism by developing the notion of a Fourth World whose inhabitants (regardless of global location) are the excluded, it is more accurate to direct attention to the other, more localized and contingent processes of inclusion and exclusion operant in all societies. These processes can be seen in the formation or reclamation of politically-laden ethnicities, hybridized racial identities, and nationalisms across the Western world. It is in this realization that Wilden's ecosystemic model is of particular assistance. From an ecosystemic perspective, the convoluted and interdependent changes to our lives and subjectivities brought about by the shift to globalization are to be expected. These interdependences have always existed, Wilden would argue, however the shift out of positivist metanarratives, which Wilden himself attempted but failed, has allowed us to recognize and begin to theorize some of these interconnections. From Wilden's perspective, this destabilization has revealed the ideological rather than the natural overlay of nation and state. It has not disappeared but it has been made visible. It has not disappeared but it has been made visible.

It is the slide from nationstate to global capitalism that has allowed, even required, these fragmented and shifting allegiances to emerge. Where nationstate capitalism required a unified, culturally homogeneous self and nation, the global capitalism which we have observed emerging requires multiple, competing and shifting selves. Guattari (cited in Stivale 1985, p. 64) has noted the connection:

> relations among individuals, groups and classes are bound up with the way individuals are manipulated by the capitalist system. Individuals as such are manufactured by that system to satisfy the demands of its mode of production.

It would be naive to misrecognize the emergence of multiple, fluid subjectivities as a release from the constraints of capitalism. This is not what is taking place. Guattari is, I believe, correct in his assertion that the types of individuals constructed within capitalist society are fundamentally linked to the needs of prevailing capitalist processes (Stivale 1985). If this is true, what we are then seeing is the shifting of the boundaries of self in response to changes in the requirements of the capitalist axiomatic. Hence, the space for new ethnic allegiances and racial identities, and the recognition of fractured, fluid and multiple subjects.

CHAPTER 8

INTERETHNICITY AND GLOBALIZATION

INTRODUCTION

Interethnicity is indeed emerging as a phenomenon—even conservative social demographers who deal primarily with country of birth statistics[28] note the shift in the racial and cultural makeup of contemporary Australia. By 1996, one in six contemporary Australian marriages were between an Australian-born and an overseas-born partner (Price 1996). In addition, the same research notes that three-quarters of second generation migrants currently marry across country-of-birth categories. Almost ten years ago, Australian demographer Charles Price predicted that by the year 2000, 40% of marriages in Australia would be cross-cultural and/or cross-racial (Price 1993). The 2001 census has just been completed across Australia and it is anticipated by many that the figures will exceed this prediction. The characteristics of the Australian population are undergoing significant shift. It is no longer adequate or acceptable to perceive of ourselves as a European outpost in the Asia-Pacific region, nor is it adequate to develop and implement economic, social or educational policies framed around narratives based on homogeneity.

THE AUSTRALIAN CONTEXT

In the Australian context—dominated by the use of sociodemographic methodologies and psychological framings of normal development—there has been a focus on ethnic and cultural difference rather than on racial identity (Luke & Luke 1998) and, as the work of Charles Price suggests, a concentration on country-of-birth as a marker of ethnic and racial descent. As Luke and Luke (1998) argue, "the main purpose in the social demography literature has been to examine historically changing in- and out- marriage rates among groups and across generations in relation to shifting 'integration' and 'assimilation' patterns" (p. 730). Thus, in general, for Australian researchers, interethnic families have existed within the 'intermarriage' category of Australian Bureau of Statistics commentaries on current demographic trends. Further, this category exists primarily as a way of judging generational maintenance of languages other than English and as a mode of tracking assimilation of new migratory groups into a pre-existing Australian mainstream (Carrington 1996). Within the sociodemographic literature these marriages are

---

[28] See in particular the corpus of Charles Price, leading Australian social demographer. Of particular interest is his more recent work (1989, 1993a, 1993b) which focuses on Asian immigration and generational patterns. As noted, Australian sociodemography is centred around categories of country-of-birth which obscure racial differences and subsume ethnic identifications. They are, in this sense, a gross instrument of measurement, but currently all that is available.

termed 'intermarriage'. Such a broad categorization acts to occlude the use of racial or ethnic categories, a situation exacerbated when we consider generational differences—regardless of how they identify themselves (Roy, Parimal & Hamilton 1993; Roy & Hamilton 1994; Stephan & Stephan 1989), the offspring of immigrants fall within a generic 'Australian' category. Consequently, with the exception of methodological (Gray 1987, 1989; Jones 1991, 1994; McCaa 1989) and interpretive (Dyer 1988; Roy & Hamilton 1994; Roy, Parimal & Hamilton 1993) disputes, Australian research has not been interested in chronicling the intermixing of the various ethnic communities identified in the multicultural literature, nor has it any interest in foregrounding the incidence of cross-racial marriage. Interethnic families remain somewhat invisible.

The growth of interethnic marriage in this country[29] would suggest, however, that rather than migrants *assimilating* into a homogeneous mainstream, this new form of racial and cultural existence—regardless of whether these are first, second or third generation 'Australians'—is *becoming* the mainstream. And, this mainstream is heterogeneous. Indeed, the sociological usefulness of the notion of a 'mainstream' is itself passing into obsolescence. Visions of Australia which focus on ethnic and racial homogeneity are out of touch with the reality of population change (Carrington 1996). Various critical analyses of this sociodemographic survey work have been conducted in relation to the politics surrounding multiculturalism and issues of gender (Bottomley 1992; Castles, Kalantzis, Cope & Morrissey 1994). Yet, public policies and debate, however well intentioned, which focus on issues of multiculturalism, have not absorbed the complexity of contemporary Australia's rapidly hybridizing racial and cultural profile.

Researchers in America and the United Kingdom have also noted the emergence of interethnicity as a phenomenon, many referring, for example, to the 'browning' of America. However, the historical trajectories of these two societies has meant that current research is dominated by issues of interracial marriage and these categories are couched in the terminologies of social psychology and identity formation (Funderburg 1994; Root 1992a, 1992b; Stephan 1992) or family therapy and counselling (Axelson 1985; Kerwin & Ponterotto 1995; Ponterotto, Casas, Suzuki & Alexander 1993). The potentially complex cultural dynamic is often reduced in these accounts to explanations of individual deficit or dysfunction (see, for example, Hudson 1998) while popular media attempt to address these issues by giving space to personal accounts (for example the quarterly magazine *Interrace: In our own words*)[30].

---

[29]   As I noted, this growth is speculated from reading between the lines of the intermarriage statistics available from the Australian Bureau of Statistics and from the information collected during the three years of the *Interethnic Families* project.

[30]   The advertising for *Interrace* claims it to be the "the first and only magazine for and about interracial couples, families, singles and people" with "articles on interracial dating and marriage, race relations, raising multiracial children and coping with society—topics you want to read about!" As well, *Interrace* offers "products for sale, personal ads for singles, an annual interracial living guide, and social events". Offshoots include *Bi-racial Child* and *Child of Colors*. In March 1999, the first issue

While the US and the United Kingdom have framed these families in terms of a normative 'scientific' discourse, in Australia we have attempted to defuse racialized categories by focusing on sociodemographic country-of-birth measures. Neither approach has the capacity for framing issues of interethnicity, particularly in connection to the changing patterns of lived existence and identity which accompany the flow of new economies. Interethnicity is becoming one of the defining trends of this era, yet the implications of this phenomenon have received limited attention. The rapidly growing interethnic population has yet to be adequately represented in sociological theory. Multiculturalism has been bypassed by the processes of globalization, while traditional theorizations of family have been so entwined with the normative requirements of the nationstate and that particular type of capitalism that they are no longer applicable. Interethnic families are representative of the shift away from this previous social world. By understanding the implications of the interethnic phenomenon we go a long way towards a theorization of family appropriate in relation to new forms of capitalism—a theorization that does not presume cultural and racial homogeneity.

A GENERATIONAL SHIFT

Like any other social groupings, interethnic families resist homogeneous representation. There is no one characteristic interethnic family. What this group has in common is its decision to form long-term family commitments across sanctioned cultural and racial boundaries. With this in mind, I believe that we can usefully identify a generational divide in the experiences of interethnic families in Australia. This generational divide, I will argue is closely connected to changes in capitalism and its demands for particular types of citizens. Research conducted in Australia (Luke & Luke 1998; Luke & Carrington 2000) for the Australian Research Council funded study *Interethnic Families Project* indicated that the experiences of peoples now in their 50s or older differs significantly from those who are recently forming interethnic relationships[31]. This older generation of interethnic couples experienced substantial disapproval from the people and the social institutions around them. We can gain an insight into this disapproval by delving into the experiences of a number of these families.

Fordist generations

Many of the families interviewed in relation to the *Interethnic Families* were older, characteristically consisting of an Anglo-Celtic husband and non-Anglo wife. All of the people interviewed in the age group—50s plus—were married and had been for

---

of *Multiface*, directed at multiracial women is due for release. Its pre-publication advertising reads, "You wished...You searched...now, we're here for YOU! Celebrate your beauty, spirit and style - IN EVERY ISSUE. Fitting in has never been easier!"

[31]   These interethnic families were interviewed during the three years of the *Interethnic Families* qualitative research project, headed by Carmen Luke and Allan Luke from the University of Queensland. V. Carrington was Project Coordinator.

many years. Many had met overseas and returned together to make a life in Australia. For many, the experience had been, at times, problematic. All of them recounted experiences of discrimination, of loss of friends and family. One Anglo-Celtic gentleman, now retired, remembered the reaction of his immediate superior to the news of his interethnic marriage to a Papuan woman:

> You have done a very foolish thing. You'll never be able to succeed you know...You've ruined your career, you've ruined your life.

Another, now late-middle aged couple, felt the disapproval of colleagues:

> And in fact one gentlemen, once I married it affected him greatly....He was dead against it...He was very polite about it but what he told other people got back to me and it was very hurtful.

> (Anglo-Australian male married to an Aboriginal-Malay woman)

Another colleague also demonstrated disapproval at this transgression of racial boundaries:

> There was a white gentlemen that I used to do business with up there and he used to go to a lot of the conventions I used to go to....and he picked us up for dinner and drove us miles away to a very secluded restaurant and sat with his back to the people.

Another younger man in his late-thirties recounted the discrimination he encountered when applying for jobs. Over the telephone he was taken to be white and, on one occasion, led to believe that he had an excellent chance of obtaining work only to be swiftly dismissed when he turned up in person and was found to be Indo-Asian. He later found out that a white man with lesser qualifications and experience was given the position.

Linked to this official displeasure and the rejections of friends and colleagues, these families felt the actuality of legal discrimination. Talking of his former wife's refusal to allow him access to their children, one man remembers back to the 1960s:

> And we went to lawyers...trying to get access to them [the children]...And they said, "Oh no...you won't win that. There's no way you would win a judgement. The judge would just throw it out".

> (Anglo-Celtic man married to a Papuan woman)

Adding to their social isolation, not only did these couples endure the disapproval and sanction of friends and colleagues and difficulties with the legal system, but also family pressure:

> I think my family's position was that they didn't think it was a good idea, um, and there was a fair bit of pressure. Oh yeah yeah, no they, you know, that they didn't think it was appropriate, and my mother made a comment I remember at the time she didn't want half-castes for children and I never forgot that, you know.

Yes, most of my friends had problems with it. They would say, "Why do you want to marry her? Why are you letting the Indian community down?"

(South African born Indian male)

These individuals experienced first-hand the reluctance or flat out refusal of friends and family to give approval to a transgression of racial lines. 'Half-caste' was a derogatory term and its use by a close family member, someone from whom you anticipate support, was undoubtedly traumatic and hurtful. The pressure of "community" expectation is also evident here—accusations of "letting the community down" are also meant to indicate that a line has been crossed, that your behaviour is not acceptable. These earlier families, even those who are now only in their mid- to late-thirties, formed across the normative sociocultural boundaries of Western Fordist capitalism while they were still policed by a conjoined nationstate and its narratives. These are the normative principles which constructed and maintained the particular imagined community of the nation—principles which focussed on the primacy of the culturally and racially homogeneous nuclear family; which stressed the notion of homogenous and place-bound community; which divided labor within this phase of capitalism primarily according to sex; and which designated and policed appropriate gender identities and roles. These are the principles, the processes of symbolic violence, which have been inherent in traditional theories of the family and they can be seen in action in these memories. In earlier Chapters, I identified this as a process of oedipalization and situated it historically within a particular phase of capitalist expansion. As a consequence of their refusal of this narrative, this generation of interethnic families endured business colleagues who felt they had the right to offer professional condemnation or who felt the need to have dinner in places where they would not be recognized, who sat where other diners could not see them eating with a mixed race couple; close family members who talked of 'half-caste' children, hinting at the shame which this would bring on the family; and a legal system which demonstrated the isolated position of these families by deeming them to be a lost cause. These people paid a high price for their transgression.

The fast capitalist generation

Interethnicity in contemporary Australia is a qualitatively different phenomenon. It draws, I believe, from a shift away from the normative principles that the older generation visibly challenged. The shift of these norming agendas is linked, I have speculated, to changes in the shape and modus operandi of capitalism. This newer generation of interethnicity, then, demonstrates a fundamental shift in the parameters of identity, nation and family.

Ethnicity, Hall (1992) suggests, responds to globalization by reinventing itself in either of two ways, 'tradition' or 'translation'. The process of translation "is a syncretistic response in which groups that inhabit more than one culture seek to develop new forms of expression that are entirely separate from their origins"

(Waters 1995, p. 137). On the surface, we can frame interethnicity in terms of translation. Hall originally devised this notion to explain the emergence of 'black' identity which has acted as a conceptual and subjective framework for peoples across various parts of the world to reinvent themselves. However, interethnic families are of interest specifically because of their creation of long-term family forms *across* ethnic and racial identities. So, while in one sense they are embodiments of Hall's translation, they also represent other, more interesting, facets of the processes of globalization. The interethnic families forming in the late 1990s, then, are an articulation of the complex and often contradictory processes which spiral out from the globalizing of capitalism.

Interestingly, and unlike older families, this new generation of interethnic families believe themselves to be just like any other. And increasingly they are, but only because the normative screening system which would previously have marginalized and sanctioned them has altered. As one partner in an interethnic relationship explained it:

> There...might be a perceived difference, but I don't think there is an actual difference anywhere...we know white-and-white couples, we know interracial couples and we are all the same. I mean there's really no difference.

This sentiment was echoed by others:

> Umm I think that everybody is seeing themselves as Australian and I don't think that race is an issue anymore.

Here the shifting of normative discourses away from the oedipalized nationstate vision of 'family' is most obvious. Like their predecessors, these families are visibly different—from each other and from other families in the local, place-bound community—and yet, for increasing numbers of these families, issues of racial and ethnic difference, which are often nationally specific constructions, are subsumed within larger globalized patterns. Of particular interest is the identification as 'Australian', which was seen as a supracategory of natural identity that overrides racial or cultural identity. In this comment, and others like it, there are markers of the response of nationstates to shifts in capitalism—an emergent discourse of reasserting homogeneous national identity in the face of a threatening world culture.

These families do not live idyllic lives free from incidents of racial discrimination, however, they do not live with this as a defining characteristic of their experiences—individually or as a family. This emerging generation of interethnicity, couples in their early to mid-twenties, believes itself to be accepted, to experience minimal sanction, and to be very much like others of their generational cohort. It appears also that this sense of acceptance and relative immunity from social sanction is shared by new immigrants of this age group. As one young Timorese-Chinese immigrant noted in relation to the response his interethnic relationship elicited:

> I didn't get very many reactions from my friends. Nor did I get any feeling that they disapproved or anything. It was more of a very easy progression. I didn't hear anything, any kind of response at all.

His partner, a young woman, originally from a small rural area, probed for unease but found none:

> I'd always asked my family you know, what do you think of Enrico? Isn't he nice? I mean, all this kind of stuff I was saying. But no, there was never any real...never any negative kind of comments.

In fact, many of these couples do not indicate any understanding of the possibility of social sanction or estrangement. Many of them know and mix with other interethnic couples of their own age. They know and went to school with many other children of mixed descent. They live in a very different world than interethnic families of an earlier generation, those who began their relationships within a community formed in the oedipalized currents of nationstate capitalism. Any of the cultural differences brought to the relationship are seen as a bonus, as a marker of positive difference from their age and social cohort and as a couple they set out to create a new familial culture—a process akin to Hall's notion of translation.

The one area of commonality remains an initial reluctance on the part of some parents when confronted with the news that their son or daughter intends to marry across cultural and racial boundaries. A number of this younger generation have carried out the initial stages of their courtship in secret, wary of parental response:

> I felt really bad going out with him and not telling them [parents] who I'm going out with. And I always had to stay outside the door to meet him and I just feel really bad. Only my sisters know.
>
> (Vietnamese female)

> For a long time everything was very secretive. We actually went out for five years before we got married so it was a long time. Nothing could have prepared him [father] for me telling them that. Well, I didn't actually tell them, he found out we were seeing each other.
>
> (Italian-Australian female married to a Vietnamese)

It is difficult to judge if any initial parental displeasure is linked to their child's choice of partner or to their decision to establish such a serious relationship in secret. Once the relationship has been made public and proven serious, parental disapproval appears to be quickly overcome:

> And that was very hard but once we started to get a little bit of support it really made a world of difference. Like we go over there for dinner quite regularly, and I am a daughter, not a daughter-in-law, I am a daughter now and that makes me feel very good.

> But slowly but surely, you know, we were basically in his face and he had to accept it, and he did. And now he thinks the world of him.

> Their reaction to us getting married? Well, when we announced the engagement,
> everything was great then. When we first went out, just at first Mum wasn't too sure,
> but then she came around so they were really good actually. I think we didn't have any
> troubles, put it that way.

(Australian-Polish male married to a Vietnamese woman)

These couples and their parents noted that the infusion of new cultural beliefs and
practices has enhanced the lives of all. Some kinds of difference are now an asset.
This is a very different response to that experienced by older interethnic couples as
they were abandoned and isolated. The generational differences highlighted in these
comments, demonstrate a shift away from the normative principles of the nationstate
overlay. The increasing tendency of this new generation of interethnic families to
view themselves as the same as everyone else highlights absences in state normative
discourses along with changes in the flow of symbolic violence. These absences are
themselves significant. These families are no longer 'different' in the eyes of the
state. In fact, in the eyes of the state, they do not exist as a specific subcultural group
or as a category. There is an absence in relation to these families. This is an
important point and I will return to it. The change of tone in recounts of experience
between interethnic families which formed in the 1950s and 1960s and those
forming now demonstrates that the agenda of racial and cultural homogeneity—the
parameters of the imagined community—has shifted for some reason.

Absence

As the experience of an earlier generation showed, the normative parameters of
Fordist society were relatively immobile and vigilantly policed. However, a key
feature of the contemporary landscape of interethnicity has been the absence of a
normative framing which specifically identifies and frames this formation.
Interestingly, with the shift to globalizing capitalism in mind, we can note that the
meaning of absence is shifting. Where an older generation of interethnic families
experienced absence as a social sanction or exclusion, this is no longer necessarily
the case. Increasingly, the racial and cultural makeup of family groupings is
irrelevant. This increasing irrelevance is directly proportional to the shifting
normative boundaries which accompany the shift to globalized capitalism. This
absence has allowed, firstly, the relatively unremarked emergence of a new
generation of interethnicity, and secondly, it has allowed these families and
individuals to construct themselves other than in relation to an oedipalizing family
narrative which acted as a synchromesh[32] in the service of the Fordist-Keynesian
nationstate.

Previous Chapters have identified Fordist-Keynesian principles of normativity and
then chronicled the shift out of this period. What I am describing here is a situation
where the state is so late in creating and authorizing a discursive framework in

---

[32]   synchromesh: a system of gears which acts to synchronize the actions of various parts and their
       speed.

which to position interethnic families (e.g. census, institutional recognition, sociodemographic mapping) that we can talk about a delayed or absent form of normativity. But, beyond this, the absence I have identified marks a shift away from the hegemony of the oedipalized symbolic violence of the nuclear narrative and all that it presupposes about identity, community and nationstate. The absent state is not a new observation. Seeking the emergence of new cultural constraints in the absence of old, Touraine (1981, p. 2) argues, "we are entering a society which has neither laws nor foundations, which is no more than a complex of actions and social relations". The differing experiences of the new generation of interethnic families testify to this. The common theme here is that the construction of social realities and of individuals to inhabit them is not disappearing, rather, that different realities and subjectivities are being formed in response to shifts in capitalism. Where previously, absence was a potent social sanction, it now marks a change in priority, a shift in the processes of symbolic violence. Thus, where the imagined community or narrative of the family was once fundamentally linked to and policed by the state, this is no longer necessarily the case. Interethnic families are a particular case in point. No clinical-therapeutic literature, no social welfare or government policy, no commercial or media discourse exists which identifies, let alone attempts to norm, interethnic families or identities. In fact, in a time of fascination with difference, interethnicity has the potential to be an advantage.

Multiculturalism and pluralism remain the dominant discourses, locked in battle with continuing calls for assimilation[33], while all are, in the final analysis, premised upon unwieldy and outmoded understandings of ethnicity, community and migration. While conservative thinkers and politicians are embarked upon a highly problematic agenda of family reconstruction, where 'family' is understood as nuclear family, the official sociodemographic literature signals the rapid increase of 'intermarriage' across all categories (Price 1993a). Interethnic families have no visible position within these debates and further, their emergence as a phenomenon cannot be satisfactorily described or theorized from within a paradigm premised upon homogeneous, static categories. The type of authority the state necessarily exercised over its citizenry to make industrial capitalism work is no longer necessary for the type of capitalism that predominates the late 1990s. This is obvious when we look at the emergence of new national and ethnic identities and the formation of family groups which skate around the normative nuclear discourse. Regardless, it would be a nonsense to argue that these normative principles have no cogency in the late 1990s. Patently they do. And there are social groups, including families and individuals who remain constructed by the half-life of Modernist social narratives. However, there are increasing sections of the social and cultural landscape in which they no longer exact the same outcomes—interethnic families are one manifestation of this shift.

---

[33] Here we cannot ignore the impact of Pauline Hanson's One Nation Party and its calls for cutbacks to immigration and the assimilation of any new migrants into what it still regards as a white, english-speaking mainstream.

The primary normative mould and the primary vehicle for analysis has been, and continues to be, the oedipal family narrative. The only categorization system with which to associate family has been the nationstate sponsored nuclear narrative. From within this paradigm, interethnic families are at risk of being framed in terms of dysfunction, and this was indeed the experience of the Fordist generations. These groupings do not fit within the parameters of the narrative—they are not culturally or racially homogeneous and by breaking this principle they also challenge the sexual and gender stereotypes which accompanied the nuclear myth. In their movement away from the white, heterosexual social order these families embody a destabilization of the patriarchal social order which has underpinned nationstate, community and family.

Implications of the interethnic phenomenon

While an older generation of interethnic families can be analyzed in terms of their crossing of cultural and racial boundaries, the new generation of interethnicities are representative of this and much more. In part they are representative of our new understanding of heterogeneity and the reality of disembedded imagined communities. But their importance as a group goes beyond this. They embody the shift in normative principles away from nationstate towards the requirements of globalizing capitalism.

It would be naive to assume that the choice of interethnicity is apolitical. These families are choosing to represent, to construct, themselves in particular ways. In this they represent Hall's (1992, 1996) descriptions of a politics of representation. They are a performative discourse which, legitimated by the requirements of globalizing capitalism, overrides nationstate primordia or paranoia. It would be no less naive to suggest that prejudice and discrimination on the basis of ethnicity or race have disappeared in the shift to a new generation. In fact, one of the short-term outcomes of globalization has been the resurgence, in some areas, of overtly racist public rhetoric. The recent emergence, in Australia, of Pauline Hanson's One Nation[34] and the vitriolic public debate it sparked, is but one example. However, these younger couples in various parts of Australia have themselves indicated that racism has had a limited impact on their lives. In part this is a result of the sites in which they live and because they represent a growing demographic pattern, but also because they choose not to make it a part of their discourse. Their capacity to make and operationalize this choice cannot be disconnected from processes of symbolic violence and constructions of habitus and is linked to changes in the normative principles generated by globalizing capitalism in New Times.

---

[34]   Pauline Hanson's One Nation Party was launched in April 1997. Her political platform directed itself at the core of resentment evident in some sections of Australia. She targeted aid for Aboriginals, non-discriminatory immigration, multiculturalism and generally lamented the disappearance of white dominated patriarchal hegemony.

It is, of course, problematic to talk about the breakdown of homogeneous categorization systems and at the same time to theorize about the significance of 'interethnic families' as a phenomenon. This would indeed be a problem if I were trying to assign a common set of practices or identities. However, this is not the point. These families are of interest because they embody a movement away from the normative principles which underpinned nationstate capitalism and, in turn, traditional theorizations of family and community. These families represent a movement beyond Appadurai's (1990) suggestions of the globalization of primordia. Appadurai theorizes this global shift in terms of group identification, and yet interethnic families represent two sides of this process. On the one hand, one partner in each interethnic family (remembering here that 'interethnic' refers to families both cross-racial and cross-cultural) is demonstrably part of the globalization of racial and ethnic identity. But, on the other hand, these families represent a choice to move outside the normative parameters that have traditionally defined the relative significance of the various primordia. And in this they are choices about the construction of identity and subjective position. The fact that these kinds of choices can be made, and are increasingly being made as differing racial and cultural groups meet on the wings of globalization, is indicative of a repositioning of these norms in New Times. However, globalization and its processes do not deliver a utopic sanctuary. Interethnic families, as well as all other families, are formed within particular currents of symbolic violence—the particular normative principles sourced in the current phase of capitalism. If this is the case, then the new generation of interethnic families are a visible marker of a shift from old principles to newly emergent ones. This is where their primary sociological significance lies.

GEOGRAPHIES OF INTERETHNICITY

When we turn to interethnicity as a contemporary phenomenon, the picture of emergent ethnicities and nationalisms in the wake of a weakening of the overlay of nation and state becomes even more complex. Not only are people in Westernized societies moving out of local, permanent communities and yet managing to maintain social relationships—what has been termed 'disembedding'—they are riding the tide of social and cultural transformation in New Times and new economies. As a demographic phenomenon, this new generation of interethnic families are visible instances of the formation of families according to new principles—a movement away from the normative principles and machines of nationstate capitalism and a Keynesian social order. Further, I believe that by examining this group we can find much of interest and relevance to a theorization of the larger concept of family within a changing socioeconomic landscape.

While not addressing the implications or reality of interethnicity, Castells (1998) has nevertheless recognized the shifts in lived experience for many people living within contemporary capitalism. In particular, Castells (1998) has noted the crisis of the nuclear family. By his account, the move to an Information Society, inextricably interwoven with the processes of globalization, has challenged the patriarchal family order. He calls it a "crisis of patriarchalism" (1998, p. 348) and makes links to the disintegration of the patriarchal family model. In Castells' view, the patriarchal family—the cornerstone of a patriarchal society:

> is being challenged in this end of the millennium by the inseparably related processes of the transformation of women's work and the transformation of women's consciousness. Driving forces behind these processes are the rise of an informational, global economy, technological changes in the reproduction of the human species, and the powerful surge of women's struggles, and of a multifaceted feminist movement, three strands that have developed since the late 1960s (1998, p. 135).

While Castells has here concentrated on the impact of feminism on Western society, I wish to take this in another direction. As Castells himself notes (1997), the problematization of patriarchy has begun to alter the ways in which people identify themselves and with others. Men, in large numbers, are increasingly willing and expected to participate more fully in the emotional and material lives of their children and partners. New gender roles require a redefinition of sexuality, argues Castells (1997), and as a consequence legitimate sexual identities have been increasingly available since Feminist theory problematized heterosexuality as a societal and human norm. The result of this challenge is the replacement of family connections by personal networks where "individuals and their children follow a pattern of sequential family, and non-family, personal arrangements throughout their lives" (1998, p. 348). Writes Castells, "nowadays, people produce forms of sociability, rather than follow models of behavior" (1998, p. 349).

Here is the link to a new sociology of the family: this sense of personal networks fits more closely with the notion of family as a fluid and dynamic social formation I wish to suggest. It suggests the performative and intentional nature of these relationships. It also allows for other non-nuclear characteristics and processes to be included rather than acting as markers of exclusion[35]. Castells, while focussing specifically on the impact of feminist theory on the awareness of women and the legitimation of non-heterosexual identities, has identified the problematization of the homogeneous nuclear family narrative. Here is the link to interethnicity. The destabilization of this myth is increasingly shifting the normative boundaries of contemporary life, and as a consequence, making a space for interethnicity as well as other non-nuclear forms of family life.

This will be a theorization that has moved away from anthropological or representational visions of 'culture' and from traditional understandings of the role of 'family' in society and in nationhood. A conceptualization of family in New Times will locate this social formation within the dynamic flows of globalizing capital and shifting currents of identity formation. Interethnic families, in their contemporary manifestation, demonstrate the loosening of the overlay between

---

[35]   Television shows such as *Seinfeld* and *Friends* clearly mirror the trend towards forming social networks that focus on friendship and common interest rather than biological connection. This has not gone unremarked in popular culture. See, for instance, David Dale's commentary in *The Courier Mail,* Saturday August 1, 1998.

nation and state and out of this, changing notions of nation. As well, they are a group who are constructing ethnicity and identity within the symbolic violence of globalization. Viewed in this way, interethnic families are a litmus test of a sociology of the family that is relevant in a globalizing world.

CHAPTER 9

GLOBALIZATION, FAMILY AND COMMUNITY

INTRODUCTION

Globalization has become a force to be reckoned with. Its impact on our lives and the ways in which we understand the world has been palpable. This could not have been foreseen by social theorists of the 1970s. From their position in the centre of a nationstate focussed modernist, it would have been impossible to predict the impact that globalizing capitalism would have on the nationstate as an ideological entity and on the social narratives which accompany it. The change in status of the nationstate resulting from the processes of globalization has become so marked that Appadurai (1990) goes as far as to suggest a new dysjunctive relationship between the nation and the state. Matters have become so "that state and nation are at each's throats, and the hyphen that links them is now less an icon of conjuncture than an index of dysjuncture" (Appadurai 1990, p. 304).

As we saw earlier, it should not be inferred from this that the notion of nation is now under threat. On the contrary, the very idea of 'nation' is expanding exponentially within globalizing capitalism. Where nation—the imagined community[36]—and state—the institutional and physical political configuration—were seamlessly overlaid within nationstate capitalism[37], the shift away from this phase has had significant impact. Wilden's ecosystemic logic would argue the inevitability of this destabilization and applaud the sudden visibility of two separate systems which had been ideologically misrepresented as one. It should be noted that the evolution of the homogeneous nationstate is not an anomaly. It represents one stage on the history of the flow of capitalism, and, according to Featherstone (1990, p. 6) "was itself an idea which became rapidly globalized". For the state, the intensification of globalization has required a new range of responses, for example, the dismantling of the welfare system and tariff protection, chronic unemployment, deregulation, and changes in regional security issues and tactics. For the nation, however, the issues have been of identity and belonging, with ramifications for what had been considered unshakeable notions of community, family and nation. In the

---

[36] Anderson (1991) used the term "imagined community" to explain the nature of the 'nation'. Anderson argued that the nation is imagined on a number of levels: members can only imagine all the other members; the nation is itself imagined as limited and sovereign. It is also imagined as a community because "regardless of the actual inequality and exploitation that may prevail in each, the nation is always conceived as a deep, horizontal comradeship" (p. 7).

[37] McGrew (1997, p. 5) notes that "modern democratic theory and democratic politics assume a symmetrical correspondence between the democratic political community and the modern nation-state" which he describes as "self-contained, self-governing" and "territorially delimited".

disengagement of nation and state, new national affiliations and ethnicities are emerging in all areas.

Thus, rather than a direct challenge to the nationstate, or a significant decrease in its significance, it is the overlay of nation and state[38] that is increasingly destabilized within the global axiomatic. Consequently, while it remains a crucial player in international relations, economics and everyday life, much of this contemporary influence is mediated via larger processes. Where previously the nationstate—and here I mean the ideologically overlaid systems within Fordist capitalism—was the primary source of the normative discourses of family, self and community, the increasing fluidity and impact of globalizing capitalism has co-opted this role. I suggest that the normative principles which are influential in designing the shape and function of the family in New Times, are sourced in a global capitalism rather than in the nationstate. Thus, globalization has acted to separate nation and state and to present each with a set of specific challenges. The result has been the problematization of the role of state and notions of nation[39].

There is a direct tie between the agenda and requirements of nationstates in terms of security and economic development, and the normative narratives which encompass family construction and life in Western societies. Earlier, I made use of High Modernist theory to critique traditional theories of the family, arguing that they have been based upon the primacy of an oedipal social order inseparable from the requirements of Fordist capitalism. I then argued that Fordist capitalism has morphed into a globalizing axiomatic. Social theorists of the 1970s, as I outlined earlier, aggressively critiqued existing normative agendas, however they did so within the framework of nationstate capitalism. Our experience and reference to current research tells us unequivocally that this is no longer the dominant form of capitalism. How, then, should we understand the changes which globalization has wrought on the nationstate in terms of family? To begin to answer this question, I turn to the ways in which we now need to frame community. This, I believe is an essential starting point in a theorization of family in New Times. I believe this to be so because the notion of family has been clearly linked with that of community, and beyond, to nation. I have suggested that the nationstate is undergoing a period of instability and reformation in response to changes in the flow and character of capitalism. This evolution is, in turn, visited upon many of the social narratives that have been closely associated with the nationstate, including community, ethnicity, race and family.

---

[38] Hobsbawm (1992) has argued that there has been a conscious attempt to overlay ethnicity-state-nation-government within the modern nationstate. Waters (1995) identifies this in terms of common identity, political system, community and administration.

[39] Like Castells (1998) I believe that the notion of 'nation' as a sense of shared history as well as shared cultural practices predates the modern nationstate. However I would argue that the advent of the modern nationstate initiated the construction and policing of a particular national identity. This is an ideological construct and it is this sense of nation that is in the process of separating from the nationstate.

GLOBALIZATION AND COMMUNITY

The breakdown of the primary relationship between state and nation has resulted in a situation where the state can no longer depend upon a normative vision of the imagined national community. This is not to declare the nuclear narrative dead. While the normative principles, symbolic systems and many other aspects of nationstate capitalism have an indefinite half-life, an increasing number of families are not formed in the shadow of the nationstate, and consequently, are not locked into the particular constructions which constituted the nuclear narrative. Without this normative frame, and in the emergence of new national and transnational communities (Hall 1992, 1996; Robertson 1992, 1995), the nationstate and all that it represents are increasingly problematized. It is in this destabilization and the reformation of normative principles that the concept of 'family' can become more inclusive of racial, cultural and sexual difference. Interethnic families are key markers of this process in the Australian context. This Chapter explores basic concepts for a new theorization of family—community, symbolic violence and glocalization.

IMAGINED COMMUNITY

In traditional theorizations—those premised upon the primacy of the nationstate—the notion of community is linked to spatial position, to locality. Themes of local community have been evident in research across the Western world. Empirical research detailing life within urban and rural sites in the United Kingdom (Young & Willmott 1962; Stacey 1960) and the United States (Zorbaugh 1929; Lynd & Lynd 1937; Dollard 1957) has built a strong facade of the 'local community'. As Albrow (1997) has noted, the notions of self, community and culture traditionally underlying post-World War Two sociological analyses can no longer be accepted without challenge. For Albrow (1997, p. 37) this movement "shifts the parameters of national economies and forces governments to attend to intangible 'supply side' factors like skills, motivation and national culture". Additionally, the meanings of migration as well as citizenship, community and locale have been problematized. Migrants—individuals or groups—no longer shift solely from one place to another and settle permanently. People are increasingly shifting across multiple locations for varying lengths of time, moving in and out of numerous communities while at the same time maintaining satisfactory social relations across all these sites (see, for example, Appadurai 1990; Castells 1996, 1998). These moving populations are not just composed of migrants or guest workers moving from one part of the globe to another, either voluntarily or involuntarily. Although this trend is notable, people are also moving from locale to locale within the same city or region, or, as globotourists travelling through and across locations for pleasure or as refugees fleeing unhappy local or national circumstances. For whatever reasons, people are on the move both globally and locally as never before, challenging traditional framings of static and homogeneous community.

The increasing movement of large groups of people in concert with the growing sophistication of communication technology has enabled the maintenance of social relations without the necessity of assimilation into local culture. Indeed, we are moving away from the belief that there is one local culture into which newcomers assimilate. Thus, migration can no longer be seen as a one-way trip to a new home and community can no longer be linked solely with the local and the place-bound. The implications of this fundamental change, what has been termed 'disembedding', are far-reaching. Of particular interest is the problematization of the local, of community. If the central argument of this text is correct, and there are primary links between concepts of the unitary self, homogeneous community, family and the nationstate, then the destabilization of the nationstate will lead, inevitably, to a destabilization in these other social narratives. This is already the case. Albrow, Eade, Dürrschmidt and Washbourne (1997) identify the recent shift from place-bound and solid communities within static values and systems of practice to the "abstract, imagined community" (p. 24) that has accompanied the processes of globalization. From their experiences in the United Kingdom they describe the imagined community of second-generation Bangladeshis living in the East End of London. The multiple identities of this group are maintained via a spread of multi-levelled connections sustained by available technologies (telephone, internet, video, television, print media). What is particularly interesting is that these imagined communities of Bangladeshis exist parallel to white and other communities in the same areas. In a time of cheap and relatively unmonitored access, the internet has become the site of many global communities ranging from chatroom mother's communities through to highly political anti-globalization groups. These people meet and maintain relationships in hypermedia sites rather than physical and localized sites. Locale, therefore, has ceased to determine the nature and extent of community. We are increasingly identifying ourselves in relation to "simulated communities" (Crook, Pakulski & Waters 1992) that make use of available technologies to pursue common agendas regardless of fractured physical presence. These are, however, *real* communities, maintaining and extending social relations across time and space—in this, they move beyond simulation. As Albrow et al. note, "community is in the process of being disembedded...to the extent that we identify its reconstitution on a non-local, non-spatially bounded basis" (1997, p. 25).

The notion of imagined community is increasingly useful in an historical moment where the nation-state entity is fragmenting and there is a growing disembedding of community from the constraints of location. As the Bangladeshi community demonstrates, there is never one homogeneous community inhabiting a particular site, and the various communities that co-exist do so across time and space via the technologies of globalizing capitalism. It is in this sense that they are imagined. My usage of the term "imagined communities" refers, then, to those communities that base themselves around particular constructed identities rather than shared location. These new community affiliations may be located within a delineated spatial zone in which they co-exist with other communities, or they may be spread across the globe. Either way, the strict sense of a sole homogenous, site-specific community inherent in older social theories is no longer adequate. Changing conditions have required that this notion be expanded to recognize the existence of synchronous, multi-levelled imagined communities.

Trust and allegiance

In another articulation of the impact of globalization on notions of community as place-bound and homogeneous, Waters (1995) suggests that this process has resulted in a "janus-faced mix of risk and trust" (p. 63). In an earlier historical moment, the individual and her material requirements remained within the confines of the personally known and the capacities of the local. However, on the currents of globalization each individual embarks on a project of the unknown, moving out of the security of a limited and localized community for even the most modest of daily requirements. As Waters explains this process:

> Under globalization individuals extend trust to unknown persons, to impersonal forces and norms (the 'market', or 'human rights') and to patterns of symbolic exchange that appear to be beyond the control of any concrete individual or group of individuals. In so doing they place themselves in the hands of the entire set of their fellow human beings (1995, pp. 64-65).

The known and trusted community has ceased to exist in these conditions, becoming increasingly disembedded and stretched across greater distances and interests. Imagined communities—which do not rely on physical proximity—are emerging around these new ways of being.

This said these community allegiances remain constructed and politicized. This should not be forgotten. Globalization has not delivered Utopia. Instead, in the wake of globalization and the decoupling of nation and state, differing normative parameters come into play as traditional narratives wane. Arguing that imagined communities and the processes of symbolic violence which create them are increasingly global rather than local, Appadurai (1990, p. 306) notes that:

> the central paradox of ethnic politics in today's world is that primordia (whether of language or skin color or neighbourhood or of kinship) have become globalized. That is, sentiments whose greatest force is in their ability to ignite intimacy into a political sentiment and then locality into a staging ground for identity, have become spread over vast and irregular spaces, as groups move, yet stay linked to one another through sophisticated media capabilities.

With this sentiment, Appadurai foregrounds the highly politicized nature of imagined communities in New Times. Again, the point here is that while the normative discourses which shaped the narratives of the nationstate are increasingly problematized, this does not mean that we have entered a time without symbolic violence and an agenda aimed at constructing specific habitus. We are entering a time when these processes are shifting, when the normative principles are (re)forming in line with the requirements of globalizing capitalism. Accompanying the dismantling of many nationstate-oriented conceptual frames and the differing requirements of a global axiomatic of its citizenry, we are seeing the decline of the essentialist unitary self. New, multiple and often contradictory subjective positionings can now be entertained. This emergence can be associated with the destabilization of the nationstate overlay. We are no longer required to see ourselves as a unitary and static individual living within a localized community within a particular physical and administrative nationstate.

How then should we conceptualize the localized sites in which we live our lives? Traditional depictions of a boundaried and homogeneous community are no longer useful and yet, regardless of images of imagined communities spreading multidimensionally across the globe and increasing geographical movement, each of us also lives in a material world. Harvey (1990) has described our experience of New Times in terms of the compression of time and space, where time has annihilated space via new technologies. Drawing upon this, Castells (1997, 1998) identifies the emergence of the Information Society and, like Hall (1992, 1996), has theorized the emergence of new identity politics. Neither of these social theorists, however, has been able to move down into the arena of everyday lived experiences and the social formations that determine them. To begin such a journey, we can draw upon the work of Dürrschmidt (1997) and Robertson (1992, 1995). Their respective concepts of 'microglobalization' and 'glocalization' are very similar in their attempt to describe the contradictory experiences of living within globalizing capitalism. They may offer new ways to envisage the localized aspect of community without retreating to older framings.

GLOCALIZATION

Transferring the global to the local without a concept of homogeneous 'community'

Dürrschmidt has taken time-space compression to have the effect that "individuals extend their scope of action and field of experience into a potentially global dimension, basically provided by access to global means of transport and communication" (1997, p. 56). What Dürrschmidt identifies is the "increased mobility and 'disembeddedness' of individual's milieux[40]" (1997, p. 57) by which he notes the increasing capacity of people to move outside traditional locations and yet maintain satisfactory contact with culture/people. This increasing fluidity of culture and individuals has impacted not only on the ways in which we perceive the global community and our individual place within it, but also on the local spaces in which we live. He defines 'microglobalization' as:

> the integration of global difference(s) and variety into a distinctive social environment. These differences refer both to humankind as such (ethnic groups, their habits, beliefs and practices) and the materializations of human activity (built environment, technologies) spatially scattered across the globe and distributed in different historical epochs. Under conditions of microglobalization these are brought together in one place, making the environment attractive for people from all over the world (p. 57).

---

[40]   Dürrschmidt (1997, p. 57) describes milieux "as relatively stable and situated configurations of action and experience, in which individuals actively generate a distinctive degree of familiarity and practical competence". He draws this understanding from the work of Grathoff (1989).

McDonald's is a classic example of this process. While, as a global franchise, demonized as the spearhead of globalization and the Americanization of global culture, each McDonald's outlet adapts itself, however minimally we might judge this to be, to the local. In Paris, the American 'Quarter Pounder' becomes the 'Royale with Cheese' and can come served with beer rather than a soft drink or shake, Norwegian McDonald's sell the McLaks (grilled salmon with dill sauce), and Thai franchises offer samurai pork burgers with teriyaki sauce (Ritzer 1998). Here we see the nonlinear nature of globalization: the homogeneity of global franchising meets the reality of local uptake and creates increased cultural choice in each localized site. In each of these sites, individuals must position this global franchise in relation to both local and distant cultures creating a push-pull effect where the global and the local intersect and overlap.

Roland Robertson (1992, 1995) has coined the term 'glocalization' to describe the relationship between the global and the local/homogeneity, and heterogeneity/universal with the particular. Globalization, according to Robertson (1995) is "not a question of *either* homogenization or heterogenization, but rather of the ways in which both of these two tendencies have become features of life across much of the late-twentieth-century world" (p. 27). 'Glocalization', then, is a way to understand this at the local level. At the moment, the term is used most widely in business, and according to Robertson (1995), was sourced in Japan where there is a long academic tradition of concern with the relationship between the particular and the universal (Miyoshi and Harootunian 1989). As Robertson notes:

> the idea of glocalization in its business sense is closely related to what in some contexts is called...micromarketing: the tailoring and advertising of goods and services on a global or near-global basis to increasingly differentiated local and particular markets (1995, p.28).

While the individual and the social formations within which she develops identity are increasingly formed in relation to the processes of global capitalism, life is still lived, for the most part, in localized sites. The concept of glocalization can go a long way toward describing the ways in which the processes of symbolic violence take effect within globalizing capitalism. Appadurai (1990) alerts us to the nature of one form of symbolic violence in contemporary globalizing societies. He writes of the exploitation by nationstates of the homogenizing tendencies of globalization:

> the simplification of these many forces (and fears) of homogenization can also be exploited by nation-states in relation to their own minorities, by posing global commoditization (or capitalism, or some other such external enemy) as more 'real' than the threat of its own hegemonic strategies (1990, p. 296).

The global citizen is linked directly to the capitalist axiomatic; lives across increasingly fluid and dynamic spatial, temporal and cultural boundaries; is increasingly likely to experience multiple displacement, of either self or family members, from place-bound community. Traditional theorizations of family are unlikely to accommodate or endorse this type of citizen. This difference can only be framed in terms of deficit or deviance from the norms of self, community and nationstate.

A new connection between identity, community and the notion of 'family' has been forged in New Times. In nationstate, industrial capitalism, the family was directly located within a spatially-bound community. Albrow and others have argued convincingly that this understanding of community is of little value within contemporary globalization, and framings such as microglobalization and glocalization attempt to capture the fluidity of social forms in this era. And, as our conceptualizations of community shift, so too must our framing of family.

NEW ETHNICITIES AND OLD FRAMINGS

From Harvey's (1990) descriptions of the economic change accompanying the shift to postmodernity we can understand the 1970s and much of the 1980s as a time of reorganization by capitalism as it morphed—spurred by localized nationstate hostilities and the breakdown of nominally socialist and capitalist ideological enclaves—deterritorializing and reterritorializing outside many of the previously established national boundaries. However, there should be no sense that globalizing capitalism has become a unified, identifiable system. On the contrary, worldwide, capitalism has taken on any number of local variants and national identities have increasingly fragmented into multiple and shifting ethnic subjectivities and political allegiances. Globalization, as I described earlier, is not a homogenizing process. It represents a shift in the direction of capitalism—a shift that has a number of sociocultural implications. An understanding of nationstate and community in the process of reconfiguration within globalization must extend to our framings of identity and ethnicity and also to family.

While the state as an institutional and physical body continues to exist, it can no longer count on a synchronous 'national' identity. This is a shared vision that is much more difficult to maintain. Globalization and the processes inherent to it have led to the emergence of specific ethnic, subjective and national identities—imagined communities—which are not constructed within the parameters of nationstate capitalism. In the emergence of these new ethnic identifications, what we are seeing is a "new cultural politics which engages rather than suppresses difference and which depends, in part, on the cultural construction of new ethnic identities" (Hall 1996, p. 446). Hall has recognized, in terms of cultural change, the shift away from an ideologically entwined nationstate towards its separation into nation and state—systems not necessarily compatible. The emergence of new ethnicities and cultural politics forms part of this process.

The processes of globalization have manifested in the notion of individualization and "the global redefinition of each person as a complete whole rather than as a subordinate part of any localized collectivity" (Waters 1995, p. 43). This means that within a globalizing society, individual and national reference points are increasingly relativized within global processes (Waters 1995). That is, we are each increasingly obliged to recognize the validity of other cultures and to position them within our overall knowledge base—as often as part of an imperative of economic viability as of an idealist categorical imperative. It is this conscious relativism that characterizes life within contemporary globalization. This is in no way a unifying process. Instead, globalization increasingly involves the "creation of a common but hyper-differentiated field of value, taste, and style opportunities, accessible by each individual without constraint for purposes either of self-expression or consumption" (Waters 1995, p. 126).

In this new landscape, ethnicity should no longer be understood as an essential characteristic of individuals or groups; rather, it is one of the multiple subject positions that individuals may inhabit. In the newly emergent configurations of globalized capitalism, 'ethnicity' as a definitive and site-specific category is increasingly problematized (Nash 1989; Omi & Winant 1986; Rattansi & Westwood 1994; Rex 1986). As Hall notes, the new politics of representation, of which ethnicity is a part, is a "process of unsettling, recombination, hybridization and 'cut-and-mix'" (1996, p. 447). 'Culture' has been problematized and ethnicity is now a marker of something other than a place-based set of exclusionary and inclusionary practices and beliefs. It accompanies newly formed framings of imagined, politicized communities and recognition of the potential for multiple subjective positioning. As with notions of nation, community and citizenship, 'culture' is increasingly fragile. Robertson (1995, p. 39) notes that:

> One of the most significant aspects of contemporary diversity is indeed the complication it raises for conventional notions of culture. We must be careful not to remain in thrall to the old and rather well established view that cultures are organically binding and sharply bounded.

It is with these older notions of culture and community that traditional theorizations of the family have been tied. In the face of the deterritorialization of these narratives, we must rethink the family.

Multiculturalism, assimilation and pluralism, regardless of their antipathy, are premised upon visions of a Modernist nationstate with its 'organic' view of culture, ethnicity and place. Regardless of good intent, the notion of 'community' which underpins these agendas remains unchanged. The retention of the fundamental premises of Modernism within the discourses of multiculturalism has been recognized by Albrow, who notes (1997, p. 37):

> One of the key aspects of the classic conceptual framework was the acceptance that place was linked to community through local culture. Migrants ultimately had to be assimilated into local culture to become part of the community. Multiculturalism put considerable stress on this framework without offering effective alternatives to older concepts of community.

Here, Albrow clearly links the discourses and rhetoric of multiculturalism into the remains of a Modernist paradigm. The conceptual and physical space of the nationstate has been premised upon homogeneities (racial, cultural, spatial)—the beginning of mass migration in the late 1950s, 1960s and into the 1970s sent social commentators and theorists scurrying for a way to frame this enormous social change. Multiculturalism stretched, but did not dismantle, the Modernist nationstate.

While the impact of non-Anglo immigration has altered the fabric of Australian society, it has tended to emerge in research and public debate as multicultural awareness of multiple separate ethnic groups (Luke & Luke 1998). From this perspective, the boundaries of 'other' have remained intact, there are just more 'others'. As a key narrative in the construction of the nationstate, the 'other' has been cast in terms of cultural, sexual and racial difference. Mired within the Modernist notion of separable nations, unified and unitary selves and an existing narrative of an internally homogeneous nationstate, these theorists described such demographic changes in terms of multiculturalism, that is, of small islands of ethnically and/or racially 'different' communities in peaceful coexistence within a larger 'mainstream' cultural background. This has never been a happy description, and contemporary research in Australia (Luke & Luke 1998) and overseas (Albrow 1997; Appadurai 1990) has convincingly problematized these boundaried cultural and racial islands, sacred territories.

This vision of a pluralistic society with neat delineations of unmixed colours is not an accurate picture of the changes that are overtaking Australia and the world. Responding to an absence of normative agendas individuals are increasingly crossing these colour and cultural boundaries. Families that are culturally[41] and racially mixed are forming in the absence created via shifting normative principles. It is these families that traditional theorizations do not accommodate, nor were they designed to. On the contrary, these were the types of social formations which nationstate narratives of community and nuclear family guarded against. What I am suggesting here is that, particularly in Australia but also in American and the United Kingdom, there is a shift, a weakening, of the normative principles that relate directly to this new family formation. This has two immediate implications. Firstly,

---

[41]   There are many who would argue that every family is culturally mixed. And this is partly true. However, families formed within and by the constraints of nationstate capitalism have been mixed within strictly monitored parameters of homogeneity. What we are seeing emerge in the late twentieth century is unprecedented family formation across racial and cultural boundaries that would have been impossible two generations ago. These are families who mix fundamental differences in racial type, religion, food and gender roles and yet who manage to create functional family formations within predominantly white institutional cultures. For these families, there is no scope for 'passing' as a nuclear family clone. A *visible* difference exists between interethnic families and other family formations and within the family itself.

we should not believe that race and ethnicity no longer matter. On the contrary, there is mounting evidence that ethnicity and race are increasingly important in a globalizing society—so important that sociological approaches to the family in New Times must explicitly incorporate them rather than resorting to psychological depictions of individual development or sociodemographic mapping. Secondly, identities are still constructed within processes of symbolic violence. This makes the establishment of a vocabulary for analysing these processes a priority.

CHAPTER 10

SYMBOLIC VIOLENCE: THE SHAPE(ING) OF THINGS TO COME

INTRODUCTION

Following on from the notion of community, an understanding of the processes that construct and maintain the narratives around which we frame our lives and beliefs is necessary. As we have seen, a new generation of interethnic families are finding themselves to be no different in many respects from other families forming within the processes of globalization. The differences inherent in interethnic families are no longer sufficiently problematic within emerging forms of globalizing capitalism to require recognition and norming. Bourdieu's sociological framing tells us that social space, in its connection to the construction of a politicized habitus, is not neutral. Thus the restructuring of space which has accompanied the shift of capitalism into a globalizing axiomatic, whether it be national, familial or personal, is inherently political and subject to forces of symbolic violence. These families are not attracting the same social sanctions as earlier generation for a reason, and party this can be explained by focussing on the nature and process of symbolic violence.

Used most potently by Pierre Bourdieu (1973, 1977a, 1977b, 1977c, 1994), the notion of symbolic violence refers to the imposition of cultural systems without connecting these practices to "the power relations which are at their source" (Bourdieu and Passeron 1990, p. 41). Remembering here that I have made use of symbolic violence to establish the explanatory potential of a generalized notion of oedipus, I believe that Bourdieu's sociological concepts have some potential in highlighting the general processes of symbolic violence which are operant in New Times. Bourdieu has quite explicitly outlined symbolic violence and its relation to the maintenance of existing hierarchies of power:

> Symbolic violence, to put it as tersely and simply as possible, is the *violence which is exercised upon a social agent with his or her complicity*....Of all forms of "hidden persuasion", the most implacable is the one exerted, quite simply, by the order of things (Bourdieu & Wacquant 1992, p. 167).

The final purpose of symbolic violence is the construction of symbolic systems which advantage particular sections of the social world. As Wacquant describes it, "to transform reality by shaping the mental schemes and meanings that guide the behaviour of those who make it up in their daily practical activities" (1987, p. 68). In addition, Bourdieu's sociological insight makes it clear that the processes of symbolic violence become embodied. Our physicality is shaped by these processes. Bodily or corporeal hexis "is political mythology realized, em-bodied, turned into a

127

permanent disposition, a durable way of standing, speaking, walking, and thereby of feeling and thinking" (Bourdieu 1991, p. 13). Thus, not only are we shaped by differing symbolic forces, but these forces become embodied.

In each generation, then, differing social and material conditions impact upon the formation of habitus and bodily hexis and a new citizen is created. The citizen of the industrial nationstate embodied a particular set of symbolic violences and as a consequence acted to recreate the symbolic systems at their source. These were focussed around the normative framings of individual, family, community and a homogeneous and boundaried nationstate. This shape reflected the relationships of the nationstate within a particular moment in the history of capitalism. As these processes shift we can expect to find a new citizen with a new bodily hexis emerging—a new habitus emerging out of the processes of globalizing capitalism. Not a generic global citizen—this is a decidedly problematic concept—but an individual whose predispositions and values and mannerisms are increasingly drawn from sources outside the nationstate.

THE NATIONSTATE RESPONSE

The nationstate is not disappearing. The dysjuncture between nation and state has not acted to dismantle the apparatus of national government. Rather, a different strategy is unfolding. We have seen evidence of this in the decline of the welfare arm of the state, the restructuring of industry and market deregulation. This process is noted by Wiseman (1998, p. 21):

> For many governments a more or less enthusiastic acceptance of the inevitability of globalization is often combined with strategies designed to maximise the competitiveness of particular national and regional economies. This commonly involves cost-cutting policies, such as labour shedding, wage reductions and deregulated labour markets, as well as measures designed to boost productivity through technological innovation and improvements in infrastructure, training, production process, marketing and distribution.

Paralleling these economic shifts and powerful public displays of control of territory (the refugee-tanker incident described in an earlier Chapter) are calls for a reconstitution of traditional family. This agenda is apparent within the rhetoric of the current Howard government in Australia.

In addition, the nationstate is harnessing the power of technology as a strategy of resistance to globalization wherein the homogenizing and destabilizing aspects of the process are foregrounded. Appadurai (1990) writes of the tendency of nationstates to use globalization to their own purposes. This connects with the shifting of normative parameters away from the nationstate, and Clarke's (1997) description of the absence of a global security agenda in the wake of the Cold War. Nationstates have no rallying call—the Soviet Union and China are no longer positioned as military threats, the homogeneous cultural boundaries of the constructed imagined community of the nationstate have demonstrably crumbled— therefore there are no immediate enemies to protect the people from and continue to justify its existence in relation to. Globalization is therefore constructed as the bad guy, as the enemy and the root of all moral decline, systemic unemployment and general unease in the community. It becomes the source of internal instabilities and the state assumes responsibility for averting violence and increased instability. The upsurge of far Right politics in this country with its agenda of racial division, reactionary social priorities and isolationist economic policies works, in this argument, to the advantage of the state.

Thus, the state (re)constructs itself as the focus of internal homogeneity in a world gone mad. As an adjunct, it produces a public rhetoric around the theme of cushioning its citizens from the negative impacts of globalization and a return to the 'good old days' of stable family and community. In this scenario, anti-globalization sentiment takes the place of Cold War anxiety, media censorship and financial regulation that were crucial to the maintenance of the nationstate overlay. In its strategy to fashion for itself the role of custodian of stability, the state harnesses the technologies of globalization to its own advantage. Here, the 1996 Australian Federal election comes to mind. While the incumbent Labor government attempted to educate the electorate to the need for economic restructuring as a response to rapidly changing global market conditions, the conservative opposition successfully seized upon, and fed, the fears and uncertainties which accompany rapid change. This message was aided by escalating interest rates during this same period—Australian home loan interest rates were over 17%. As Wiseman (1998, p. 47) describes it, "For thirteen years Labor rode the tiger of global economic restructuring while trying to prevent the beast from eating too many Australian citizens". The citizens, however, lost faith in 1996 and voted for the 'relaxed and comfortable' vision of Australia peddled by Howard, naively presuming that this was a less painful option. What they got was a neoliberal government committed to the same economic rationalist policies as those of Thatcher and Reagan in the 1980s. Translating this to a larger frame, global communications allow the construction of shared fears (for example, AIDS, Chernobyl, global warming and the destruction of the ozone layer) as well as imagined communities and a global consumer culture. The tendency of globalization to relativize the cultures and locations of peoples across the globe has fed into fears of homogenization and creeping Americanization of the world. As well, the fragmentation and local resistance which are also outcomes of globalization, too, fuel the fears of various sections of communities around the world who feel increasingly powerless and marginalized. These fears are fanned as the various mass media, driven by their own political and ideological agendas, supply the information base which is moulded into commonsense knowledges of globalization and its implications for specific locations and persons. It was this commonsense understanding and constructed fear that carried the conservative parties into government in Australia in 1996 and re-elected them three years later. Another federal election is looming. It will interesting to see the outcome.

This process is itself one of the symbolic violences of globalization as we are reconstructed to view ourselves as part of a global community rather than local or national. The shift into this type of world view is resisted by many, particularly those who believe that changes such as those they associate with globalization are personally threatening in terms of financial security or cultural hegemony. These commonsense understandings of cultural and economic change become the views we see argued in the Letters-to-the-Editor sections of newspapers, on pulp television current affairs programmes, and in the rhetoric of far right politics. The technologies of communication, now as always, are used as an agent of symbolic violence in the service of the state.

The material conditions of life

These processes are inextricably wedded to the material conditions of everyday life. The needs of capitalism create the material conditions that are then inscribed into habitus to create particular types of people. This is a self-perpetuating, yet dynamic, process. What then are the material conditions of life within globalizing capital? The new flows of symbolic violence are taking effect within a phase of capitalism wherein the individual worker can no longer expect to work in one job for a lifetime. An employment lifetime is increasingly measured in consecutive short to medium term contracts. Employment, thus, is in the process of redefinition, marking the transition out of an earlier phase. As a consequence, the new worker is expected to be increasingly mobile, following employment from site to site as the flow of capitalism shifts. The worker who is unable/unwilling to shift is abandoned. In this climate there is need for a citizen/subject who does not equate work with identity. The shifting and impermanent nature of employment opportunities requires that each citizen have an identity that exists outside that of worker. This is a fundamental change from the days when you *were* your job—a construction which acted in the interests of nationstate capitalism and rampant patriarchy.

It is here that the increasing importance of imagined communities in our daily lives and in our constructions of identity comes into play. Where once identity was ascribed on the basis of racial and cultural characteristics, gender or employment— all specifically delineated categorizations—it is now generated out of a series of imagined communities and sub-cultural groupings. These community identifications are not locked in place—they are not dependent upon homogeneous place-bound connections, and in this they compliment the need for the serial relocation of workers to reflect the increasing mobility of capital and manufacturing. Thus, for a new generation of Australians, identity is formed in relation to a broader range of influences than the Modernist criteria of racial or cultural category or local community. There is also a sense that each individual has numerous identity options which they may take up at any moment. The ability to read each social situation and recognize valued knowledge and behaviour is increasingly important. The reality and accessibility of imagined communities has provided legitimate alternatives for identity and community for a new generation.

Making the jump to capitalism and consumer culture, Massumi (1992) writes that "gender, race, ethnicity, religious practices, belief systems, beauty, health, leisure—and every other aspect of molar human existence—has been resolved into component parts: images that may be purchased by a body and self-applied as desired" (p. 135). Continuing, he notes that "you can go anywhere your fancy takes you and be anyone you want to be—as long as your credit is good, and you show for work the next day" (Massumi 1992, p. 136). For those who are able to participate in the consumption cycle of fast capitalism, identity is a malleable commodity. The designation of 'other' has shifted towards those who are so far out in the margins that there is no way back under prevailing economic and cultural conditions. One of the outcomes of an increasingly globalized capitalism is an expanding gulf between those with access to technology and skills, and those without. A 'digital divide' is opening gup around issues of access and skill, but also in relation to ageing technology (Meredith & Thomas 2000).

Interethnic families with good credit ratings, and who contribute to creating a marketable local identity, are free to design their own identities, as are others. Perhaps in a world of niche-marketing and microglobalizations we are creating niche-people or niche-identities. However, we should not be fooled—these fluid and niched persons are created and have relevance within the symbolic violence of globalizing capital. Marcuse (1956) would link this shift to the need for capitalist society to "defend itself against the spectre of a world which could be free" (p. 93). This defence is mounted via our coerced willingness to participate in the production-consumption flow. As Marcuse observes:

> if society cannot use its growing productivity for reducing repression (because such usage would upset the hierarchy of the *status quo)*, productivity must be turned *against* the individuals; it becomes itself an instrument of universal control (1956, p. 93).

The increasing commodification of identity, in this view, is one of the systems of control—one of the processes of symbolic violence. Schor (2000) identifies a "new consumerism" where consumption becomes part of identification with a reference group. The difference between this activity and the notion of 'keeping up with the Jones'" (who generally lived in our local community and had a similar income) lies in the disconnection between income and consumer desire—the movement of our aspirations beyond the boundaries of our earning ability. Commodification of identity becomes part of the aspiration cycle. We want to belong to a 'better' reference group and the way to look as though we do is to purchase consumer goods. The mass media portray a range of upper middle class and upper class models of consumption and identity for us to aspire to. Schor argues that we have experienced a "rapid escalation of desire and need, relative to income" and further, that this goes a long way to explaining the huge rise in credit card and other personal debt and an accompanying fall in family and personal savings since the mid-80s (2000, p. 2). Identity commodification, in this view, is part of the process of symbolic violence characteristic of life in new economies.

Localized sites

Space, as a physical presence, is not unconnected to the development and implementation of subjectivity. Within globalizing capitalism with its increasing fluidity of identity and the increased physical movement of persons across the globe, the importance of space has not lessened. In a time of fluid and fickle capital, Castells (1996) notes that the space of flows is global while the space of place is local. And, in fact, the processes of globalization have turned our attention to space with new intensity. In this new world of rapidly diverting currents of capital, information, images and bodies, geographical location is becoming a key contributor to life pathway. Edgar (1999, pp. 6-7) notes that "the life chances of Australians now depend even more heavily on regional location, inequality in incomes reflects a complex interaction between educational skill levels and geographic industry section concentration". Life pathways and identity are linked closely to the local, but do not exist outside the impacts of the global. This is the push-pull effect of glocalization. Massey and Jess (1995), in their human geography, equate globalization with changing subjective categorizations of space. For them:

> Globalization is the process by which the relatively separate areas of the globe come to intersect in a single imagined 'space'; when their respective histories are convened in a time-zone or time-frame dominated by the time of the West; when the sharp boundaries reinforced by space and distance are bridged by connections (travel, trade, conquest, colonization, markets, capital and the flows of labour, goods and profits) which gradually eroded the clear-cut distinction between 'inside' and 'outside' (1995, p. 190).

This is not entirely accurate. There will always be insiders and outsiders—Bourdieu's sociology argues quite clearly that social space is stratified, contested and dynamic. What we are experiencing is the increasing ephemerality of what were once considered timeless categories and boundaries, many of which I have identified as part of the hegemony of nationstate capitalism. Normative agendas that differentially advantage and disadvantage have not disappeared, rather they are increasingly fluid because, increasingly, they are sourced outside the parameters of the nationstate. The qualities of various locales must be vigorously advertised in order to attract investment and production opportunities which determine access to employment and a decent standard of living. Here then is an impetus for the increasing differentiation of place as part of an ongoing economic strategy (see Harvey 1990). David Mulford, one time United States Under Secretary of State, cynically noted that, "the countries that do not make themselves attractive will not get investors' attention. This is like a girl trying to get a boyfriend. She has to go out, have her hair done up, wear make up" (cited in Wiseman 1998, p. 61). Notwithstanding the unspoken assumptions about gender and patriarchy, Mulford is making a clear connection between investment, desire, and exploitation.

The key points here are that globalization carries with it systems of symbolic violence which are acting to construct particular social realities. These symbolic systems are inscribed onto our very bodies creating, if we are to believe Bourdieu, bodily hexis and habitus-directed daily activities which will act to advantage particular social groups. Taking place, then, is the shift from construction of citizens for a world composed of strictly policed and relatively autonomous nationstates to the construction (and for some sectors of society, the *re*construction) of a new citizen whose habitus is in tune with the shape of capitalism in New Times.

Turning to the significance of interethnic families in such a time of flux, new generations of interethnic families are not formed within the symbolic violence of oedipalizing relationships, nor do they assimilate into a homogeneous cultural 'mainstream'. The very notion of a 'mainstream' society, Australian or other, assumes the existence of a core, homogeneous culture, maintained by processes of assimilation. The existence of this new generation of interethnic families problematizes this assumption. These families invent and maintain site- and family-specific ethnicities and practices—heterogeneities. And, as I noted earlier, the mainstream is itself heterogeneous. Increasingly, these families are disembedded and yet able to maintain satisfactory social networks across time-space—the notion of community against which they, in practice, reference themselves, is not limited to delineated localized sites. Like the rest of us, they are caught up in the pressures of increased aspirations that accompany the weakening of local community ties. This system of normative currents is no different for interethnic families than for any other form of family in this phase of capitalism. Thus the observations of young interethnic couples that they are no different to any other couples are accurate. The primordia which acted against this form of marriage in an earlier generation no longer carry the same normative weight. The imperatives of globalizing capitalism have shifted the weightings of various mechanisms of exclusion and inclusion. Consequently, identity and inclusion as a citizen or a family no longer rest upon these same normative principles.

CHAPTER 11

LANDSCAPING 'FAMILY'

INTRODUCTION

Given the changes in social processes and the material conditions of life identified here, how can we begin to frame family in a way that has relevance in New Times? No longer is it appropriate to draw upon narratives of oedipalized gender, sexual and role stereotypes. Nor is it possible to assume any type of practical homogeneity. In this final section I begin to trace the outlines of an appropriately fluid conceptualization. This draws upon the work of Appadurai and Albrow, but also takes into account materialist understandings of the connection between cultural life and the material processes in which it takes shape.

As the nationstate reshapes itself in relation to a new phase of capitalism, the family cannot but be reshaped in the eddies created by the delinkage of nation and state. Where in traditional theorizations of family the connection between nationstate and family (understood in relation to a narrow band of 'normal' roles and practices) was taken for granted, this can no longer be the case. To restate, nuclear family— premised upon a particular set of symbolic violences and oedipal relationships—was directly connected to Fordist capitalism and the accompanying ideological overlay of nation and state. The shift of capitalism into a new phase, that of globalization, has problematized firstly, the nation-state union and secondly, all the various normative agendas such as family, sexuality and identity which underpinned it. This shifting environment calls for, and creates, a new type of citizenry and a new set of subjective positionings. Consequently, new normative processes evolve and take shape. Thus, the space of the nation, the family and the individual are all in flux—in movement away from the normative agendas of an earlier capitalism.

We have already explored the broad outlines of the forces which mitigate towards the construction of a new citizen-worker. This shift emphasises the need to rethink how we theorize 'family'. Traditional frameworks presuppose the industrial-Fordist citizen and community, yet I have argued that this community is *passé* and that this citizen is under renovation. The 'family', exposed in the critiques of theorists such as Wilden and Deleuze and Guattari as one of the primary clamps holding together these two systems, must now be revisited in light of the disengagement and destabilization I have described. Regardless of how we might view the changes which the evolution of capitalism have wrought, we are in need of a way to theorize our social life which is relevant and appropriate in a period of systemic flux.

Scapes

The very notion of the Western 'family' is linked fundamentally and inextricably to patterns of oedipalized symbolic violence. Appadurai's (1990) formulation of the notion of 'scapes' is more useful at this juncture, particularly as he has formulated it in relation to a destabilization of the ideological nationstate conjuncture. Appadurai suggests that contemporary society can be explained more appropriately by reference to the concept of a 'global cultural economy' which is "sustained by the disjunctures between cultural, political and economic processes" (Appadurai 1990, p. 296). He identifies five key dimensions of the global cultural flow which are emerging in the disengagement of nation and state: ethnoscapes—the shifting flow of people around the globe as migrants, refugees, tourists and guestworkers; mediascapes—the flow of media technology and information as well as the images produced; technoscapes—the increasingly fluid and rapid spread of technology across national boundaries; finanscapes—flow of global capital; and ideoscapes— shifting, politicized flow of ideologies. Appadurai believes that the new phase of globalization has destabilized economy, culture and politics (1990) and proposes that his formulation of a framework (which he describes as 'elementary') of cultural flow allows us to analyze these dysjunctures.

The term 'scapes' offers a sense of fluidity, irregularity and ultimate indeterminacy. These scapes are the source of 'imagined worlds'—"multiple worlds which are constituted by the historically situated imaginations of persons and groups spread around the globe" (Appadurai 1990, p. 296-7). Thus the notion of scapes allows the move away from the Modernist concepts of community and neighbourhood which, as Albrow (1997) points out, have been made redundant within the processes of globalization. In addition, they allow a move outside the constraints of the concept 'culture'. 'Culture', along with nationstate and nuclear family, are specifically Western creations which have acted to essentialize identity and physical location (Friedman 1995). Friedman has suggested that the concept of culture transforms difference into essence (1988, 1991, 1995). He writes:

> The most dangerously misleading quality of the notion of culture is that it literally flattens out the extremely varied ways in which the production of meaning occurs in the contested field of social existence. Most atrociously, it conflates the identification of specificity by the anthropologist with the creation and institutionalization of semantic schemes by those under study. It confuses our identification with theirs and trivializes other people's experience by reducing it to our cognitive categories (1995, p. 81).

Appadurai has attempted to address this danger through his recognition of the fluidity and perspectival nature of his scapes. The various imagined communities we construct and live within together constitute the various scapes he has identified. These various scapes combine to form 'imagined worlds'—"constituted by the historically situated imaginations of persons and groups spread around the globe" (Appadurai 1990, p. 296-7). In one of the only attempts to date to take up Appadurai's notion, Albrow (1997) has attempted to insert a structural frame around these flows by formulating the overarching concept of the 'socioscape'. Albrow is concerned to move beyond the seemingly phenomenological orientation of imagined worlds. His agenda is therefore to identify the "social formations which are more than the people who occupy them at any one time" (1997, p. 38).

Albrow's conceptualization of the socioscape is, at first glance, attractive. However, when applied to the notion of family it raises a dilemma. Albrow's reformulation of the concept of the scape forces us to decide whether to view family in New Times as an enduring social structure which exists independently of individuals or as a nebulous scape which exists only via the performative discourses and practical activities of participants. Albrow has not contested the notion of scapes—on the contrary he has sought to supplement it with this broader level of analysis. Should we view family as a socioscape, a social structure or a scape in the fluid and dynamic sense described by Appadurai? Do families exist without the people who occupy them? This has been the difficulty of Modernist framings of the family. The normative narrative has been objectified in dominant discourses, given an independent existence of its own. My position here is that the requirements of the capitalist axiomatic have undermined any notion of family as a static social structure. Inexorably, there is a movement towards the family-scape and its unlikely that revisiting the family as an enduring social structure can offer any new insight.

It is at the level of the imagined world that Appadurai locates the potential for political and ideological struggle. Albrow, I believe, would locate ideological contestation at the level of the socioscape. However, the recognition that globalization of life has not removed the processes of symbolic violence which shape each of us in particular ways makes it apparent that each of the various scapes are themselves processes of symbolic violence. They are not avenues for contesting the symbolic violence of particular constructed socioscapes. Taking this idea and moving back to the shift away from nationstate capitalism, a global citizen narrative is emerging from within the current phase of capitalism, gradually replacing the oedipalized nationstate citizen created through the narratives of Modernism. This entire process is highly politicized and linked directly to the imperatives of the dominant forms of capitalism. Currently, these are the processes of globalizing capitalism. For the moment, I wish to explore the potential of 'scapes' for reconceptualizing family.

While I am impressed by this notion I have some difficulties which I will outline before drawing upon 'scapes' in relation to reconceptualizing 'family' in a globalizing world. Appadurai has separated the field of culture from its connections with the capitalist flow and from the political currents which are also sourced in it. It is in the dysjuncture between these fields that he identifies the flow of the new global culture. For my purposes, Appadurai has not focused on the applicability of his notion of scapes to the intersections of material and social space which determine everyday life. Although in the first instance driven by the consequences of the material processes of globalizing capitalism, his theorization differentiates between culture and the material world in which it has meaning. This becomes particularly evident in his description of financscapes as "mysterious, rapid and difficult" (1990, p. 297). This does not capture the importance of capitalism in the coagulation of Appadurai's remaining scapes. While it is an important methodological distinction, I would argue that the impact of the capitalist system is immanent across and through all sociocultural formations and, moreover, it is the processes of contemporary capitalism which have created the environments Appadurai describes in terms of 'scapes'. This process has acted to problematize social theories which create distinctions between various fields. Global capitalism has subsumed such distinctions within its axiomatic and we need to theorize accordingly whenever possible. So, while Appadurai goes a long way toward providing the analytic tools with which to reconstruct our framing of family in the current evolutionary phase of capitalism, he does not go far enough.

Family as sociospace

The fluidity of 'scapes' is very attractive. Particularly when they are understood as imagined communities and worlds constructed within processes of symbolic violence lodged in the material processes of capitalism. As Wilden (1980) pointed out there are always interdependencies between the constructed human worlds—our imagined worlds—and the material conditions of life. Traditional theorizations of the family attempted to position a particular normative narrative in such a way that it acted to maintain and police the parameters of an imagined community and to synchronize the actions of this imagined community in relation to an ideologically framed set of material conditions. That is, the reality of material conditions was perceived through a set of Modernist lenses. As we have seen, these conditions have changed rapidly and fundamentally over the last ten to fifteen years. I am going to explore the possibilities of using scapes in relation to family formation within the constraints of what we would have previously referred to as material and sociocultural processes. To make this connection I am going to move slightly away from Appadurai's terminology, referring to families as 'sociospaces'. In so doing, I hope to foreground the social and material aspects of scapes. In this section I wish to outline the broad parameters of a framing of family which positions it as a sociospace. To accomplish this I am going to visit a number of characteristics of the sociospace, including its status as imagined community, its shift away from oedipalized relationships and its connections to space and place. All of these aspects derive from the material processes of globalizing capitalism—it is in the shift out of industrialized capitalism and its relationship with the nationstate entity that an increasingly fluid and ephemeral social world is emerging.

Imagined Community

The sociospace family is above all else an imagined community. It has this in common with the narrativized nuclear family. What is central to family sociospaces forming within globalization is the construction and maintenance of social bonds and of support networks. These are supplementary to, and for increasing numbers of persons, replacing the equation of biological with social connection that characterized Modernist presumptions of family. Where once it was an unquestioned social priority, people no longer necessarily assign primary value to biological family. Increasingly, as television shows and social profiles reflect, individuals are forming families-of-choice to whom they turn for emotional and financial support.

Another feature of imagined communities is their ability to establish and maintain themselves across the time-space boundaries which characterized Modernism. The technological changes which have accompanied globalization present opportunities for disembedding these relationships from place. This allows the maintenance of satisfactory and sustained social relationships outside the boundaries of local space and time. It is possible to keep in touch via email, the web, telephone or satellite link-up from anywhere in the world to anywhere else. Failing this high level of technology, ordinary mail can be delivered virtually anywhere in the world within a few days, if not overnight. Television links people across any number of places around a single audiovisual image. The point here is that sociospace families are not, of necessity, constructed or constrained within localized sites or temporal boundaries. While some of these sociospaces exist in shared sites such as houses, others exist across spaces. Members may live in other parts of the same city, in other parts of the country, or in other countries. The limits which location placed on the maintenance of the social bonds of community and family have been transcended.

What this also means is that the 'family' is no longer to be conceptualized as one of the structural pillars of the nationstate. It remains, along with other sociospaces, a key player in the operation of the social world, however it is no longer the prime mechanism for the delivery of homogeneic and patriarchal messages. There is no doubt that for the contemporary state the 'family' remains central. This 'family' is still perceived as a static entity, linked to particular economic and ideological agendas, however, this view is under constant challenge from persons demanding legitimation of their particular family form. Over the course of recent decades, the state has been forced to recognize and legitimate the existence of single parent families (and this has meant abandoning the equation of single families with single mothers), same sex families and blended families. As we saw earlier, interethnic families remain unrecognized and invisible to the substrata of the state. The trend here is a struggle between the state and its citizens to force the state to accommodate rapid change in family formation.

Post-oedipus and symbolic violence

As I have suggested, particular types of subjectivities are still produced within globalizing capitalism. Any notion of fluid sociocultural scapes must incorporate the acts of symbolic violence which create social beings. In my opinion, the family remains a key sociological formation, but I also believe that it should no longer be conceptualized in relation to an oedipalized myth drawn from nationstate politics and economic flows. If my arguments are correct, then the oedipalized narrative of identity and family is becoming a less potent social machine. Reflecting this movement, the particular sexualized relationships of the nuclear family and the traditional lens for viewing it are also left behind in a conceptualization of family in terms of sociospace. Non-heterosexual families and families-of-choice—network families—can represent themselves via the notion of sociospace where they were unable to do so from within traditional framings. The oedipal framing has been removed and non-nuclear families can no longer be labelled deficit or dysfunctional. Indeed, they are performative social discourses, strategic networks of choice which operate in and across localized sites.

Thus, this notion offers a conceptual framework in which to locate personal networks, the traditional vision of nuclear family, same-sex families as well as interethnic families. As we have done with recent conceptualizations of fluid and imprecise subjectivity we must also let go of essentialist interpretations of family. Family becomes, then, a sociospace rather than a normative machine. And, once we conceptualize family in this way it can again be a useful sociological concept. Conceptualizing family as a fluid and dynamic sociospace removes its status as a foundational and enduring social structure. It places emphasis on the activities and shared symbolic systems of people and clearly articulates a vision of individuals moving across various sociospaces in the course of a day or a lifetime. This, I suggest, is a more useful representation of family in a time of rapid change and a globalizing capitalist system.

While I am arguing that a framing of family is needed which can account for the increasing heterogeneity of life in a time of rapid globalization I am not trying to paint a picture of a future without racism and prejudice. Although previous sections noted that a new generation of interethnic families does not expect racism or discrimination to impact significantly on their lives, this does not mean that it will not. As the 1998 Queensland[42] State election demonstrated, race is re-emerging as an issue in contemporary Australian politics and as our current illegal immigration debacle demonstrates, we still have an inadequate vocabulary for debate. A framing of the family which recognizes the impact of New Times does not attempt to minimise or discount racism. What sociological reconstructions such as the one I am presenting *can* tell us is that the emergent racisms of the 1990s are not the same phenomenon as the racisms of the industrial Fordist nationstate. They are generated along differing fracture and political lines and although they coexist with the half-lives of older racisms, we need to theorize them differently. A new set of sociological frameworks which attempts to address the rapid change and currents of symbolic violence which are the companions of globalizing capitalism and the social world it is creating can go a long way towards a more useful understanding.

Space and material processes

Wilden's (1980) ecosystemic model, for all its inherent structuralisms, has much to offer an alternate framing of family. He was adamant about the interdependencies between epistemologically divided spheres of existence/reality. I believe that we

---

[42]   Queensland is a State on the eastern side of Australia.

cannot theorize family without taking account of the total immersion of each individual and each family in space—material and social.

Sociospaces necessarily exist within the physical and material world. Bourdieu's sociological framing is helpful here. The material spaces in which individuals develop habitus have a physical impact. Thus, the bodily hexis of each individual reflects, to some extent, the material conditions of her life—where she grew up in terms of accent, taste and other mannerisms, overall physical condition and appearance, her employment history. Thus the material conditions of life which globalization delivers will impact on the spaces of each individual and consequently, her social connections or sociospaces. Importantly, where the material conditions supplied by globalization differ from those of earlier phases, differing bodily hexis and habitus will result. As this analysis has outlined, globalization has delivered differing types and durations of labor, differing experiences of community and, connected to all this, new normative principles. What this means in terms of the shift away from 'traditional' family is that increasingly we are being moulded into the kind of habitus that mitigates towards fluid social formations, towards a different lived experience of family.

Like subjectivity, the ways in which people inhabit family and/or interethnicity is mediated by time and place. That is, every family experiences itself in site-specific ways. This is not new. However, what *is* new is that we are no longer bound by ideological blinkers to expect to see the nuclear family narrative objectified in day-to-day life. It has been exposed, in the decoupling of nation and state, as one of a number of normative narratives. Because I view all aspects of social life to be connected to the material processes of capitalism, it follows that the shift toward network families serves the purposes of new forms of capitalism. The habitus of a new generation of citizens are constructed within the flows of the capitalist axiomatic. These flows require that the new citizen is mobile and malleable. A static nuclear family based in a place-bound community does construct en masse this type of citizen-worker. By conceptualizing family as a sociospace I suggest there is an increasing opportunity to frame each family within site specific and shifting environments. This is a requirement of any sociological frame which makes a claim to efficacy within globalization—increasing relativism and movement require that any concept of family accommodates this ephemerality.

The notion of sociospaces takes us toward a conceptualization of fluidity and flow rather than Modernist bounded cultural spaces and normed practices. Building upon Appadurai we can begin to reconceptualize family in New Times as an open and nebulous system rather than a static machine of symbolic violence acting in concert with other social machines to create a particular range of tick-the-box identities and roles within nationstate capitalism. This framing does not represent cultural, sexual and racial heterogeneity in terms of deficit or dysfunction because, as I have noted, globalizing capitalism has a limited interest in the maintenance of Modernist understandings of homogeneity. Where traditional theorizations of family have been constrained by inherent presumptions of homogeneity and stasis, 'scapes' and 'sociospaces' have no such loyalty.

CONCLUSION

To make this argument, I have drawn, in varying degrees, upon a diverse range of literatures—Deleuze and Guattari's generalized understanding of Oedipus, Bourdieu's sociological framework, Wilden's ecosystemic logic. While my various choices may have seemed unusual, I suggest that they are entirely justified in that they have allowed me to describe the role of the nuclear family within capitalism in a particularly useful manner. Without reference to Deleuze and Guattari's notion of a generalized oedipus, and my description of it as a mechanism of symbolic violence, this analysis would not have been possible. Wilden's ecosystemic understanding provided the backdrop against which I position the material and sociocultural processes of capitalism. As well, the framing of family in New Times I have presented would not have been possible without a synthesis of the concepts of symbolic violence and Appadurai's notion of scapes. A strange, but powerful, creolization.

New times: New families has argued that the nuclear family as we have come to know it through government and church policy and mass media is not a natural nor a neutral social formation. In order to appreciated the highly politicized nature of this family it has been necessary to firstly, historicize key theoretical frames and secondly, to problematized them. Then, drawing from contemporary social theory, it has been possible to build a framework that moves away from homogeneity and older forms of capitalism. The normative principles which characterized nationstate capitalism no longer serve as universal reference points for individual lives. This is not to argue that there are no normative principles in action, but rather that these new principles differ qualitatively from those which underwrote nationstate, integrated self and oedipalized family. Across the Western world, people continue to form themselves into separate family groups living in single family dwellings. Given my arguments—firstly, that this normative family shape and function is tied directly to a particular phase of capitalism and the nation; secondly, that we are experiencing a new phase of globalizing capitalism; and thirdly, that there is a shift in the potency of the normative principles which created and maintained the oedipalized family— why is this so?

Some of these families are formed on the still existing currents of the oedipalizing nationstate—identities and roles remain shaped by uni-dimensional attitudes and belief systems. The social and cultural worlds will always be shaped by combinations of the residual and the new and by competition between the emergent and what has always been. Some families are created by different currents—these families may visibly fit the mould but the internal dynamics are increasingly complex. Other families, rather than retaining a shape (created within a normative mould) perform their shape. These families are parasitic, opportunistic. They are dynamic, performative and open rather than closed and static as they were once depicted in theory and common knowledge. They are sociospaces. Eade (1997) notes:

> the emergence of new rhetorics and practices which problematize social, cultural and political conventions shaped by nation-state structures. Attempts may well be made by white residents to incorporate 'outsiders' like 'black and Asian' settlers into a local working-class culture and community. Nevertheless, the emerging literature on hybridity, diasporic communities and new ethnicities indicates the manifold ways in which global migrants and their descendants are defying assimilation into conventional political discourses and practices. Indeed, their supra-national links enable them to challenge these conventional modes of interpreting the world within specific territories (p. 128).

This is precisely the connection I made to the rise of interethnicity as a phenomenon of note. And, this emergence is challenging the ways in which we, in the West, have traditionally formulated our notion of family. No longer is it appropriate or acceptable to reference ourselves against, and insulate ourselves in accordance with, Modernist nuclear family narratives. These narratives inherently assume patriarchal and heterosexual relationships, homogeneous cultural and racial groupings and a particular position within a Modernist industrial nationstate. In the realities of twenty-first century living, these are demonstrably no longer the primary normative principles around which society and family form. Increasingly, families are forming around networks of choice[43] rather than biological connection or cultural/racial profile. What has changed is that the narrative of the family is less and less a useable tool in maintaining an outdated and unworkable image of the nationstate. The normative principles in operation in relation to families have shifted, within the parameters dictated by globalizing capitalism, away from the oedipalizing norms which characterized the Fordist nationstate. This is clearly demonstrated in the life experiences of the new generation of interethnic families in Australia.

One of the final questions to ask is, will globalization deliver a time and space in which all imagined communities will exist without prejudice? The answer has to be: I doubt it. Interethnic families are undeniably mixed, culturally and racially. For global capitalism, this is currently an insignificant variant: for nationstate capitalism it was a very significant deviation from the normative agendas of the time. The narratives of Modernism will continue to have a significant potency, particularly for the generations whose habitus were formed within this system of symbolic violence. This is not a negative ending to this work. Rather, it is positive. There has been a shift away from this particular closed and paranoid understanding of the world and of family, and the interethnic families which are forming within contemporary

---

[43] A recent report by British social analysts for Prudential Insurance Company, *Next Generation: Lifestyles for the Future,* has predicted, amongst other things, that 'families of choice' are replacing biological family structures.

globalizing capitalism are a marker of both this shift and of the potential of the future.

REFERENCE LIST

Adams, R.N. (1960). Inquiry into the Nature of the Family. In G. Dole & R.L. Carneiro (Eds.), *Essays in the Science of Culture* (pp. 30-49). New York: Crowell.

Albrow, M. (1997). Travelling Beyond Local Cultures: Socioscapes in a global city. In Eade, J. (Ed.). *Living the Global City: Globalization as local process* (pp. 37-55). London: Routledge.

Albrow, M., Eade, N., Dürrschmidt, J. & Washbourne, N. (1997). The impact of globalization on sociological concepts: Community, culture and milieu. In Eade, J. (Ed.). *Living the Global City: Globalization as local process* (pp. 20-36). London: Routledge.

Amin, S. (1976). *Unequal Development: An essay on the social formations of peripheral capitalism* (B. Pearce, Trans.). Hassocks: Harvester Press.

Amin, S. (1977). *Imperialism and Unequal Development.* Hassocks: Harvester Press.

Amin, S. (1990). *Maldevelopment: Anatomy of a global failure.* (M. Wolfers, Trans.). London: Zed Books.

Anderson, B. (1991). *Imagined Communities: Reflections on the origin and spread of nationalism* (Rev. ed.). London: Verso.

Appadurai, A. (1990). Disjuncture and difference in the global cultural economy. In Featherstone, M. (Ed.). *Global Culture: Nationalism, globalization and modernity* (pp. 295-310). London: Sage Publications.

Arato, A. (1982). *The Essential Frankfurt School Reader.* New York: Seabury.

Ariés, P. (1962). *Centuries of Childhood: A social history of family life.* (R. Baldick, Trans.). New York: Vintage Books.

Arieti, S. (1967). *The Intrapsychic Self: Feeling and cognition in health and mental illness.* New York: Basic Books.

Ashcroft, B., Griffiths, G., & Tiffin, H. (1998). *Key Concepts in Post-Colonial Studies.* London: Routledge.

Australian Bureau of Statistics. (1996). *Australian Social Trends 1996.* Canberra: Australian Government Publishing Service.

Axelson, J. (1985). *Counseling and Development in a Multicultural Society.* Monteray CA: Brooks/Cole Publishing Co.

Bales, R. & Parsons T. (1955). Preface. In *Family, Socialization and Interaction Process* (pp.v-xi). USA: The Free Press of Glencoe.

Barrett, M. & McIntosh, M. (1991). *The Anti-Social Family.* London: Verso.

Bateson, G. (1972). *Steps to an Ecology of Mind.* New York: Ballantine Books.

Bateson, G. (1979). *Mind and Nature.* New York: E.P. Dutton.

Becvar, D. & Becvar, R. (1993). *Family Therapy: A systemic integration.* (2nd ed). Boston: Allyn & Bacon.

145

Benston, M. (1972). The Political Economy of Women's Liberation. In N. Glazer-Malbin & H.Y. Waehrer (Eds.). *Woman in a Man-Made World* (pp. 119-128). Chicago: Rand McNally.

Bentall, R. (1990). Preface. In R. Bentall (Ed.). *Reconstructing Schizophrenia* (pp. 1-3). London: Routledge.

Bertalanffy, L. von (1968). *General System Theory: Foundation, development, application.* New York: Braziller.

Bertalanffy, L. von (1975). *Perspectives on General System Theory: Scientific-philosophical studies* (E. Tashdjian, Ed.). New York: Braziller.

Best, S. & Kellner, D. (1991). *Postmodern Theory: Critical Interrogations.* Houndmills: Macmillan.

Bogue, R. (1989). *Deleuze and Guattari.* London: Routledge.

Bottomley, G. (1992). *From Another Place.* Cambridge: Cambridge University Press.

Bourdieu, P. (1973). Reproduction and Social Reproduction. In R. Brown (Ed.). *Knowledge, Education and Cultural Change: Papers in the sociology of education* (pp. 71-122). London: Tavistock.

Bourdieu, P. (1977a). The economics of linguistic exchange. *Social Sciences Information,* 16 (6), 645-668.

Bourdieu, P. (1977b). Symbolic power. In D. Gleeson (Ed.). *Identity and Structure: Issues in the sociology of education* (pp. 112-119). England: Nafferton Books.

Bourdieu, P. (1977c). *Outline of a Theory of Practice.* Cambridge: Cambridge University Press.

Bourdieu, P. (1984). *Distinction: A social critique of the judgement of taste.* (R. Nice, Trans.). New York: Routledge.

Bourdieu, P. (1990). *The Logic of Practice.* (R. Nice, Trans.). Cambridge: Polity Press.

Bourdieu, P. (1991). *Language and Symbolic Power.* (J.B. Thompson, Ed., M. Adamson, Trans.). Cambridge: Polity Press.

Bourdieu, P. (1994). Structures, Habitus and Practices. In *The Polity Reader in Social Theory* (pp. 95-110). Cambridge: Polity Press.

Bourdieu, P. & Passeron, J. (1990). *Reproduction in Education, Society and Culture.* (R. Nice, Trans.). London: Sage Publications.

Bourdieu, P. & Wacquant, L. (1992). *An Invitation to Reflexive Sociology.* Chicago, University of Chicago Press.

Boyle, M. (1990). The Non-Discovery of Schizophrenia? In Bentall, R. (Ed.). *Reconstructing Schizophrenia* (pp. 3-22). London: Routledge.

Braudel, F. (1985). *The Perspective of the World* (S. Reynolds, Trans.). London: Fontana Press.

Bulmer, M. (1984). *The Chicago School of Sociology: Institutionalization, diversity, and the rise of sociological research.* Chicago: The University of Chicago Press.

Callan, V. & Noller, P. (1987). *Marriage and Family.* North Ryde NSW: Methuen.

Cardosa, F. (1972). Dependency and Development in Latin America. *New Left Review,* 74, 83-95.

Carrington, K. (1991). Policing families and controlling the young. In R. White & B. Wilson (Eds.) *For Your Own Good: Young people and state intervention in australia* (pp. 108-117) [Special edition of *Journal of Australian* Studies]. Bundoora, Victoria: La Trobe University Press.

Carrington, V. (1996). Interethnic Families. Paper presented at the Australian Institute of Family Studies Annual Conference, Brisbane, November.

Carrington, V. & Luke, A. (1997). Literacy and Bourdieu's Sociological Theory: A reframing. *Language and Education,* 11 (2), 96-112.

Carrington, V., Mills, M. & Roulston, K. (2000). A feel for the game: Strategic deployments of masculinity. *Critical Pedagogy Networker,* Vol 13 (4), 1-11.

Castells, M. (1996). *The Rise of the Network Society.* London: Blackwell.

Castells, M. (1997). *The Power of Identity.* Malden, MA: Blackwell.

Castells, M. (1998). *The End of Millennium.* Malden, MA: Blackwell.

Castles, S., Kalantzis, M., Cope, B., & Morrissey, M. (1994). *Mistaken Identity: Multiculturalism and the demise of nationalism in Australia.* (3rd ed.). Sydney: Pluto Press.

Chodorow, N. (1989). *Feminism and Psychoanalytic Theory.* New Haven: Yale University Press.

Chodorow, N. (1994). *Femininities, Masculinities, Sexualities: Freud and beyond.* Kentucky: The University Press of Kentucky.

Chomsky, N. (1999). *Profit over people: Neoliberalism and global order.* New York: Seven Stories Press.

Christian, B. (1985). *Black Feminist Criticism, Perspectives on Black Women Writers.* New York: Pergamon.

Clark, I. (1997). *Globalization and Fragmentation: International relations in the Twentieth Century.* Oxford: Oxford University Press.

Collins, P. (1991). *Black Feminist Thought: Knowledge and consciousness, and the politics of empowerment.* New York: Routledge.

Connell, R. (1995). *Masculinities.* St. Leonards, Vic.: Allen & Unwin.

Connell, R. (1997). Men, Masculinities and Feminism. *Social Alternatives,* 16 (3), 7-10.

Crook, S., Pakulski, J. & Waters, M. (1992). *Postmodernization.* London: Sage.

Dalla Costa, J. & James, S. (1975). *The Power of Women and the Subversion of the Community* (3rd ed.). Montpelier: Falling Wall Press Ltd.

Dale, D. (1998, August 1). 50 TV Shows That Changed Us. *The Courier Mail,* pp. 1, 4.

de Beauvoir, S. (1974). *The Second Sex* (H.M. Parshley, trans. and Ed.). New York: Vintage Books.

deLepervanche, M. & Bottomley, G. (Eds.). (1988). *The Cultural Construction of Race.* Sydney: Sydney Association for Studies in Society and Culture, University of Sydney.

Deleuze, G. (1997). Societies of Control. In N. Leach (Ed.). *Rethinking Architecture: A reader in cultural theory* (pp. 309-316). London: Routledge.

Deleuze, G. & Guattari, F. (1983). *Anti-Oedipus: Capitalism and schizophrenia*. Minneapolis: University of Minnesota Press.

Deleuze, G. & Guattari, F. (1987). *A Thousand Plateaus: Capitalism and schizophrenia*. Minneapolis: University of Minnesota Press.

Delphy, C. (Ed.). (1984). *Close to Home: A materialist analysis of women's oppression* (D. Leonard, Trans.). London: Hutchinson in association with the Explorations in Feminism Collective.

Dinnerstein, D. (1977). *The Mermaid and the Minotaur: Sexual arrangements and human malaise*. New York: Harper Colophon Books.

Dollard, J. (1957). *Caste and Class in a Sourthern Town*. Garden City, New York: Doubleday.

Dowling, C. (1981). *The Cinderella Complex: Women's hidden fear of independence*. New York: Pocket Books.

Duffy, M. (1998, August 16). PM gets personal. *The Sunday Mail*, p. 5.

Dürrschmidt, J. (1997). The Delinking of Locale and Milieu: On the situatedness of extended milieux in a global environment. In J. Eade (Ed.). *Living the Global City: Globalization as local process* (pp. 56-72). London: Routledge.

Dyer, K. (1988). Changing Patterns of Marriage and Mating Within Australia. *Australian Journal of Sex, Marriage and Family*, 9 (2), 107-119.

Eade, J. (Ed.). (1997). *Living the Global City: Globalization as local process*. London: Routledge.

Eden, L. & Potter, E. (Eds.). (1993). *Multinationals in the Global Political Economy*. New York: St. Martin's Press.

Edgar, D. (1999) Learning to Live with Complexity: Social trends and their impact on Queensland education Online: http://education.qld.gov.au/corporate/qse2010/otherresearch.html#Complexity

Engels, F. (1972). *The Origin of the Family, Private Property and the State in the light of the researches of Lewis. H. Morgan*. New York: International Publishers.

Fagan, R. & Webber, M. (1994). *Global Restructuring: The Australian experience*. Melbourne: Oxford University Press.

Featherstone, M. (1990). Global Culture: an introduction. In M. Featherstone (Ed.). *Global Culture: Nationalism, globalization and modernity* (pp. 1-14). London: Sage Publications.

Featherstone, M. (1991). *Consumer Culture and Postmodernism*. London: Sage Publications.

Featherstone, M. (1993). Global and local cultures. In J. Bird, B. Curtis, T. Putnam, G. Robertson & L. Tickner (Eds.). *Mapping the Futures* (pp. 169-185). London: Routledge.

Feeley, K. (1972). *Flannery O'Connor: Voice of the peacock*. New Brunswick NJ: Rutgers University Press.

Firestone, S. (1970). *The Dialectic of Sex*, New York: Bantom Books.

Foucault, M. (1973). *Madness and Civilization: A history of insanity in the Age of Reason* (R. Howard, Trans.). New York: Vintage Books.

Foucault, M. (1979). *Discipline and Punish: The birth of the prison* (A. Sheridan, Trans.). Harmondsworth: Penguin Books.

Foucault, M. (1986a). *The History of Sexuality, Volume 2.* (R. Hurley, Trans.). New York: Vintage Books.

Foucault, M. (1986b). *The History of Sexuality, Volume 3.* (R. Hurley, Trans.). New York: Pantheon.

Foucault, M. (1997). Of Other Spaces: Utopias and heterotopias. In N. Leach (Ed.). *Rethinking Architecture: A reader in cultural theory* (pp. 350-355). London: Routledge.

Frank, A.G. (1991). The Underdevelopment of Development [Special issue]. *Scandinavian Journal of Development Alternatives,* 10 (3).

Freud, S. (1972). The Psychology of Women: Biology as destiny. In N. Glazer-Malbin & N.Y. Waehrer (Eds.). *Women in a Man-Made World* (pp. 55-61). Chicago: Rand McNally.

Freud, S. (1995). The Dissolution of the Oedipus Complex. In P. Gay (Ed.). *The Freud Reader* (pp. 661-666). London: Vintage.

Freud, S. (1995). Civilization and Its Discontents. In P. Gay (Ed.). *The Freud Reader* (pp. 722-772). London: Vintage.

Friedman, J. (1988). Cultural logics of the global system. *Theory, Culture and Society,* 5 (2/3), 447-60.

Friedman, J. (1991). Further notes on the Adventures of Phallus in Blunderland. In L. Nencel & P. Pels (Eds.). *Constructing Knowledge* (pp. 96-113). London: Sage Publications.

Friedman, J. (1995). Global System, Globalization and the Parameters of Modernity. In Featherstone, M., Lash, S. & Robertson, R. (Eds.). *Global Modernities* (pp. 69-90). London: Sage Publications.

Fromm, E. (1955). *The Sane Society.* New York: Rinehart.

Fromm, E. (1970). *The Crisis of Psychoanalysis.* New York: Fawcett.

Funderburg, L. (1994). *Black, white, other: Biracial Americans talk about race and ethnicity.* New York: William Morrow.

Giddens, A. (1991). *Modernity and Self-Identity.* Cambridge: Polity Press.

Gilding, M. (1997). *Australian Families: A comparative perspective.* Melbourne: Addison Wesley Longman.

Gillman, C.P. (1966). *Women and Economics.* New York: Harper & Row (Original work published 1898, under the name C.P. Stetson).

Gladding, S. (1995). *Family Therapy: History, theory and practice.* Englewood Cliffs, N.J.: Merrill.

Goode, W.J. (1963). *World Revolution and Family Patterns.* New York: The Free Press.

Goode, W.J. (1971). A Sociological Perspective on Marital Dissolution. In M. Anderson (Ed.). *Sociology of the Family* (pp. 301-320). Harmondsworth: Penguin Books.

Goody, J. (Ed.). (1971). *Kinship.* Harmondsworth: Penguin Books.

Goody, J. (1983). *The Development of Family and Marriage in Europe.* Cambridge: Cambridge University Press.

Goody, J. (1996). *The East in the West.* Cambridge: Cambridge University Press.

Gray, A. (1987). Intermarriage: Opportunity and Preference. *Population Studies, 41,* 365-379.

Gray, A. (1989). Measuring Preference for In-Marriage: A response to McCaa. *Population Studies, 43,* 163-166.

Grosz, E. (1990). Feminism and Anti-Humanism. In A. Milner & C. Worth (Eds.). *Discourse and Difference* (pp. 63-75). Monash University: Centre for General and Comparative Literature.

Guha, R. & Spivak, G. (Eds.). (1988). *Selected Subaltern Studies.* New York: Oxford University Press.

Gunew, S. (1994). *Framing Marginality: Multicultural literacy studies.* Carlton, Victoria: Melbourne University Press.

Gunew, S. & Yeatman, A. (Eds.). (1993). *Feminist Knowledge: Critique and construct.* New York: Routledge.

Habermas, J. (1973). *Legitimation Crisis* (T. McCarthy, Trans.). London: Heinemann.

Habermas, J. (1979). *Communication and the Evolution of Society* (T. McCarthy, Trans.). Boston: Beacon Press.

Hall, S. (1992). Questions of Cultural Identity. In S. Hall, D. Hold and T. McGrew (Eds.). *Modernity and its Futures* (pp. 274-316). Cambridge: Polity.

Hall, S. (1996). New ethnicities. In D. Morley & K. Chen (Eds.). *Stuart Hall: Critical dialogues in cultural studies* (pp. 441-449). London: Routledge.

Haralambos, M. (1980). *Sociology: Themes and perspectives,* UK: University Tutorial Press Limited.

Haralambos, M., van Krieken, R., Smith, P. & Holborn, M. (1996). *Sociology: themes and perspectives* (Australian edition). Melbourne: Longman.

Hartmann, H. (1979). Capitalism, patriarchy, and job segregation by sex. In Z.R. Eisenstein (Ed.). *Capitalist Patriarchy and the Case for Socialist Feminist* (pp. 206-247). New York: Monthly Review Press.

Harvey, D. (1990). *The Condition of Postmodernity.* Cambridge, MA: Blackwell.

Harvey, D. (1996). *Justice, Nature & the Geography of Difference.* Cambridge, MA: Blackwell.

Held, D. (1995). *Democracy and the Global Order: From the modern state to cosmopolitan governance.* Cambridge: Polity Press.

Herrnstein, R. & Murray, C. (1994). *The Bell Curve: Intelligence and class structure in American life.* New York: Free Press.

Hirst, P. & Thompson, G. (1996). *Globalization in Question.* Oxford: Polity Press.

Hobsbawm, E. (1992). *Nations and Nationalism since 1780* (2nd ed.). Cambridge: Cambridge University Press.

hooks, b. (1981). *Ain't I a Woman: Black women and feminism*. Boston: South End Press.

hooks, b. (1989). *Talking Back: Thinking feminist, thinking black*. Boston: South End Press.
hooks, b. (1992) *Black looks: Race and representation*. Boston: South End Press.

Hopkins, T. & Wallerstein, I. (Eds.). (1996). *The Age of Transition: Trajectory of the world system 1945-2025*. London: Zed Books.

Horkheimer, M. (1982). The End of Reason. In A. Arato & E. Gebhardt (Eds.). *The Essential Frankfurt School Reader* [reprinted from *Zeitschrift* 9, (1941), 366-388] (pp. 26-48). New York: Seabury.

Horkheimer, M. & Adorno, T. (1987). *Dialectic of Enlightenment* (J. Cumming, Trans.). New York: Continuum.

Howard, J. (1996). Transcript of Speech at the Launch of the Family Tax Initiative, Wentworthville, Sydney. 16th December, 1996. [On-line]. Available: http://www.pm.gov.au/aword/

Hoyte, G. (1997, April 17). A Trip to The Temple. *Semper*, 3, 14-15.

Hudson, I. (1998) Mixed Messages: Prejudice and interracial couples *Interrace*, 42, 14-17.

Irigaray, L. (1991). *The Irigaray Reader* (edited and with an introduction by M. Whitford). Cambridge MA: Basil Blackwell.

Ironmonger, D. (Ed.). (1989). *Households Work: Production activities, women and income in the household economy*. Sydney: Allen & Unwin.

Jackson, P. (1993). Towards a cultural politics of consumption. In J. Bird, G. Curtis, T. Putnam, G. Robertson & L. Tickner (Eds.). *Mapping the Futures: Local culture, global change* (pp. 207-228). London: Routledge.

Jay, M. (1973). *The Dialectical Imagination: A history of the Frankfurt School and the Institute of Social Research 1923-50*. London: Heinemann.

Jones, F. (1991). Ethnic Intermixture in Australia, 1950-52 to 1980-82: Models or Indices? *Population Studies*, 45, 27-42.

Jones, F. (1994). Are Marriages that Cross Ethnic Boundaries More Likely to End in Divorce? *Journal of the Australian Population Association*, 11 (2), 115-132.

Joseph, G. (1984). Black Mothers and Daughters: Traditional and new perspectives. *Sage: A Scholarly Journal on on Black Women*, 1 (2), 17-21.

Jureidini, R., Kenny, S. & Poole, M. (Eds.). (1997). *Sociology: Australian Connections*. St. Leonards, NSW: Allen & Unwin.

Kellner, D. (1984). *Herbert Marcuse and the Crisis of Marxism*. London: Macmillan.

Kellner, D. (1989). *Critical Theory, Marxism and Modernity*. Cambridge: Polity Press.

Kellner, D. (1991). Introduction. In H. Marcuse *One Dimensional Man* (pp. xi-xxxix). (2nd ed.). London: Routledge.

Kerwin, C. & Ponteretto, J. (1995). Biracial identity development: Theory and research. In J.G. Ponterotto, J. Casas, L. Suzuki & C. Alexander (Eds.) *Handbook of Multicultural Counselling* (pp. 199-217). Thousand Oaks: Sage Publications.

152 REFERENCE LIST

Klein, M. (1975a). *Narrative of a Child Analysis: The conduct of the psycho-analysis of children as seen in the treatment of a ten-year old boy.* London: Hogarth Press and the Institute of Psycho-Analysis.

Klein, M. (1975b). *The Psycho-Analysis of Children.* (A. Strackey, Trans.). London: Hogarth Press and the Institute of Psycho-Analysis.

Laslett, P. (1972). Mean Household Size in England since the Sixteenth Century. In P. Laslett (Ed.). *Household and Family in Past Time* (pp. 125-158). Cambridge: Cambridge University Press.

Lee, R. (1996). Structures of Knowledge. In T. Hopkins & I. Wallerstein (Eds.). *The Age of Transition: Trajectory of the world system 1945-2025* (pp. 178-206). London: Zed Books.

Lévi-Strauss, C. (1969a). *The Elementary Structures of Kinship* (J. Bell, J. von Sturmer & R. Needham, Trans.). Boston: Beacon Press.

Lévi-Strauss, C. (1969b). *The Raw and the Cooked.* (J. & D. Weightman, Trans.). New York: Harper and Row.

Lévi-Strauss, C. (1973). *From Honey to Ashes* (J. & D. Weightman, Trans.). London: Cape.

Levy-Bruhl, L. (1975). *The Notebooks on Primitive Mentality* (P. Riviere, Trans.). Oxford: Blackwell.

Leys, C. (1996). *The Rise and Fall of Development Theory.* London: James Currey Ltd.

Luke, A. & Carrington, V. Globalisation, literacy, curriculum practice (in press/2001) Chapter for: R. Fisher, M. Lewis & G. Brooks (Eds), *Language and Literacy in Action.* London: Routledge/Falmer.

Luke, C. & Carrington, V. (2000). Race Matters. *Journal of Intercultural Studies.* Vol 21 (1) pp. 5-24.

Luke, C. & Luke, A. (1998). Interracial Families: Difference within difference. *Ethnic and Racial Studies,* 21 (4), 728-755.

Luke, T. (1995). New World Order or Neo-World Orders: Power politics and ideology in informationalizing glocalities. In M. Featherstone, S. Lash, & R. Robertson, R. (Eds.). *Global Modernities* (pp. 91-107). London: Sage Publications.

Lynd, R. & Lynd, H. (1937). *Middletown in Transition: A study in cultural conflicts.* New York: Harcourt Brace.

Marcuse, H. (1956). *Eros and Civilization: A philosophical inquiry into Freud.* London: Routledge & Kegan Paul.

Marcuse, H. (1964). *One-Dimensional Man.* London: Routledge.

Marginson, S. (1997). *Markets in Education.* St. Leonards NSW: Allen & Unwin.

Massey, D. & Jess, P. (Eds.). (1995). *A Place in the World? Places, Cultures and Globalization.* Oxford: The Open University.

Massumi, B. (1992). *A User's Guide to Capitalism and Schizophrenia: Deviations from Deleuze and Guattari.* Cambridge MI: The MIT Press.

Massumi, B. (1997a). *Realer Than Real: The simulacrum according to Deleuze and Guattari.* [On-line]. Available: http://www.uq.edu.au/~enbmassu/first-and-last/works/realer.htm.

Massumi, B. (1997b). *The Politics of Everyday Fear: Everywhere You Want to Be.* [On-line]. Available: http.www.uq.edu.au/~enbmassu/first-and-last/works/feareverywhere.htm

Mattingly, P. (1997). The Suburban Canon Over Time. In P. land & T. Miller (Eds.). *Suburban Discipline* (pp.38-51). New York: Princeton Architectural Press.

Mead, G. (1934a). (edited and with an introduction by C.W. Morris). *Mind, Self, and Society: From the standpoint of a social behaviorist.* Chicago: The University of Chicago Press.

Mead, G. (1934b). (edited and with an introduction by A. Strauss). *The Social Psychology of George Herbert Mead.* Chicago: The University of Chicago Press.

Mead, M. (1943). *Coming of Age in Samoa: A study of adolescence and sex in primitive societies.* London: Penguin.

Mead, M. (1961). *Coming of Age in Samoa: A psychological study of youth for western civilization.* New York: Morrow.

Meredith, D. & Thomas, J. (2000). Virtually no policy: Modulating the digital divide. *Southern Review.* Vol. 33 (2), 212-230.

McCaa, R. (1989). Isolation or Assimilation: A log linear interpretation of Australian marriages, 1947-60, 1975, and 1986. *Population Studies, 43,* 155-162.

McCarthy, T. (1976). Introduction. In J. Habermas, *Communication and the Evolution of Society* (pp. vii-xxiv). Boston: Beacon Press.

McChesney, R. (1999). Introduction. *Profit over people: Neoliberalism and global order,* N. Chomsky. New York: Seven Stories Press, pp.7-16.

McGrew, A. (Ed.). (1997). *The Transformation of Democracy? Globalization and Territorial Democracy.* Polity Press: The Open University.

Mikesell, R., Lustermann, D. & McDaniel, S. (Eds.). (1995). *Integrating Family Therapy: Handbook of family psychology and systems theory.* Washington DC: American Psychological Association.

Miller, D. (1973). *George Herbert Mead: Self, language, and the world.* Austin and London: University of Texas Press.

Mills, M. (1997). Boys and Masculinities in Schools. *Education Links* 54, 22-24.

Minh-ha, T. (1989). *Women, Native, Other: Writing postcoloniality and feminism.* Bloomington: Indiana University Press.

Mitchell, J. (1971). *Women's Estate.* New York: Pantheon Books.

Mitchell, J. (1974). *Psychoanalysis and Feminism.* New York: Vintage Books.

Morgan, D.J.H. (1975) *Social Theory and the Family.* London: Routledge & Kegan Paul.

Morgan, L.H. (1876). Montezuma's Dinner. *North American Review,* Vol. 122 [Reprint A0251 in Bobbs-Merrill Reprint Series in the Social Sciences].

Morgan, L.H. (1963). *Ancient Society* (Edited by Eleanor Burke Leacock). New York: World Publishing Company.

Murdock, G. (1949). *Social Structure.* New York: Macmillan.

Miyoshi, M. & Harootunian, H.D. (Eds.). (1989). *Postmodernism and Japan.* Durham: Duke University Press.

Nash, M. (1989). *The Cauldron of Ethnicity in the Modern World.* Chicago: University of Chicago Press.

Negri, T. (1988). *Revolution Retrieved: Writings on Marx, Keynes, capitalist crises and new social subjects (1967-1983).* London: Red Notes.

Noller, P. & Fitzpatrick, M.A. (1993). *Communication in Family Relationships.* Englewood Cliffs, NJ: Prentice Hall.

Oakley, A. (1974). *The Sociology of Housework.* New York: Pantheon Books.

Oakley, A. (1976). *Housewife.* Harmondsworth: Penguin Books.

Oakley, A. (1982). *Subject Women.* London: Fontana.

Olsson, K. (1998, August 22). Women split over family value. *The Courier Mail,* p. 26.

Ogbu, J. (1987). Variability in minority school performance: A problem in search of an explanation. *Anthropology and Education Quarterly* 18 (4), 312-334.

Omi, M. & Winant, H. (1986). Racial Formation in the United States: From the 1960s to the 1980s. New York: Routledge.

Ortner, S. (1975). Oedipal Father, Mother's Brother, and the Penis: A review of Juliet Mitchell's "Psychoanalysis and Feminism". *Feminist Studies* 2 (2/3), 167-182.

Osmond, M. & Thorne, B. (1993). Feminist Theories: The social construction of gender in families and societies. In P. Boss, W. Doherty, R. LaRossa, W. Schumm & S. Steinmetz (Eds.). *Sourcebook of Family Theories and Methods: A contextual approach* (pp. 591-622). New York: Plenum Press.

Palmer, G. (1978). Dependency: A formal theory of underdevelopment or a methodology for the analysis of concrete situations of underdevelopment? *World Development 6,* 881-924.

Parsons, T. (1955). The American Family: its relations to personality and to the social structure. In T. Parsons & R. Bates (in collaboration with J. Olds, M. Zelditch & P. Slater). *Family, Socialization and Interaction Process* (pp. 3-33). Glencoe, Illinois: The Free Press of Glencoe.

Parsons, T. (1977). *The Evolution of Societies* (Edited and with an introduction by Jackson Toby). NJ: Prentice-Hall.

Pieterse, J. (1995). Globalization as Hybridization. In M. Featherstone, M., S. Lash & R. Robertson. (Eds.). *Global Modernities* (pp. 45-68). London: Sage Publications.

Ponterotto, J., Casas, J., Suzuki, L. & Alexander, C. (Eds.). (1995). *Handbook of Multicultural Counselling.* Thousand Oaks CA: Sage Publications.

Price, C. (1989). The Melting Pot is Working. *IPA Review,* 42 (3), [December 1988-February 1989], 34-35.

Price, C. (1993a). Ethnic intermixture in Australia. *People and Place,* 1 (1), 6-8.

Price, C. (1993b). Australia as intermediary with Asia: a demographic view. *Journal of Intercultural Studies,* 14 (1), 19-32.

Price, C. (1996). Ethnic intermixture of migrants and indigenous peoples in Australia. *People and Place*, 4 (4), 12-16.

Rattansi, A. & Westwood, S. (Eds.). (1994). *Racism, Modernity and Identity: On the Western front*. Cambridge: Polity Press.

Reifer, T. & Sudler, J. (1996). The Interstate System. In T. Hopkins & I. Wallerstein (Eds.). *The Age of Transition: Trajectory of the world-system 1945-2025* (pp. 13-37). London: Zed Books.

Reiger, K. (1991). *Family Economy*. Victoria, Australia: McPhee Gribble.

Reiger, M. (1985). *The Disenchantment of the Home: Modernizing the Australian family, 1800-1940*. Melbourne: Oxford University Press.

Rex, J. (1986). *Race and Ethnicity*. Milton Keynes: Open University Press.

Ritzer, G. (1998). *The McDonaldization Thesis*. London: Sage Publications.

Robertson, R. (1992). *Globalization, Social Theory and Global Culture*. London: Sage Publications.

Robertson, R. (1995). Glocalization: Time-space and homogeneity-heterogeneity. In M. Featherstone, S. Lash and R. Robertson (Eds.). *Global Modernities* (pp. 25-44). London, Sage Publications.

Root, M. (1992a). Within, between, and beyond race. In M.P. Root (Ed.). *Racially Mixed People in America* (pp. 3-11). Newbury Park: Sage Publications.

Root, M. (1992b). *Racially Mixed People in America*. Newbury Park: Sage Publications.

Roy, P. and Hamilton, I. (1994). Patterns of Intermarriage in Australia: Regional variations in intermarriage rates. *Australian Journal of Marriage and Family*. 15 (3), 124-136.

Roy, P. Parimal, J. and Hamilton, I. (1993). *Intermarriage in Australia: A comparison of intermarriage rates in Gippsland and the rest of Australia*. School of Humanities and Social Sciences, Monash University Gippsland Campus.

Sachs, J. (1998). Globalization and Employment: a public lecture. International Institute for Labour Studies, International Labour Organization [On-line]. Available: http://www-ilo-mirror.who.or.jp/pu.

Sarantakos, S. (1996). *Modern Families*. Melbourne: Macmillan Education Australia Pty. Ltd.

Schor, J. (2000) The new politics of consumption: Why Americans want so much more than they need. *Boston Review. [On line] Available: http://bostonreview.mit.edu/BR24.3/schor.html*

Seem, M. (1983). Introduction. In G. Deleuze and F. Guattari, *Anti-Oedipus: Capitalism and schizophrenia* (pp.xv-xxiv). Minneapolis: University of Minnesota Press.

Sieghart, M. (1998, August 1). 1950s Man needs an update. *The Australian*, p. 13.

Spivak, G. (1990)). *The Post-Colonial Critic: Interviews, strategies, dialogue*. New York: Routledge.

Sprengnether, M. (1995). Mourning Freud. In A. Elliott & S. Frosh (Eds.). *Psychoanalysis in Contexts: Paths between theory and modern culture* (pp. 142-165). London: Routledge.

Stacey, M. (1960). *Tradition and Change: A study of Banbury*. London: Oxford University Press.

Stephan, C. (1992). Mixed-Heritage Individuals: ethnic identity and trait characteristics. In M. Root (Ed.). *Racially Mixed People in America* (pp. 50-63). Newbury Park: Sage Publications.

Stephan C. & Stephan, W. (1989). After Intermarriage: Ethnic identity among mixed-heritage Japanese-Americans and Hispanics. *Journal of Marriage and the Family,* 51 (2), 507-519.

Stivale, C. (1985). Pragmatic/Machinic: Discussion with Félix Guattari. 19th March 1985. [On-line]. Available: http://www.dc.peachnet.edu/~mnunes/guattari.html.

Stratton, J. (1998). *Race Daze: Australia in identity crisis.* Annandale, N.S.W: Pluto Press.

Strauss, A. (1934). Introduction. G.H. Mead, G. *The Social Psychology of George Herbert Mead* (pp. iv-xvi). Chicago: The University of Chicago Press.

Szasz, T. (1974). *Ideology and Insanity: Essays on the psychiatric dehumanization of man.* Harmondsworth: Penguin.

Szasz, T. (1994). *Cruel Compassion: Psychiatric control of society's unwanted.* New York: Wiley & Sons.

Thatcher, M. (1995). *The Path to Power.* London: Harper Collins.

The Frankfurt Institute for Social Research. (1972). The Family. In *Aspects of Sociology* (pp. 129-147). Boston: Beacon Press.

Thompson, L. & Walker, A. (1995). The Place of Feminism in Family Studies. *Journal of Marriage and the Family,* 57, 847-856.

Tong, R. (1989). *Feminist Thought: A comprehensive introduction.* Boulder, Colorado: Westview Press.

Touraine, A. (1981). *The Voice and the Eye: An analysis of social movements* (A. Duff, Trans.). Cambridge: Cambridge University Press.

Touraine, A. (1995). *Critique of Modernity* (D. Macey, Trans.). Oxford, UK: Blackwell.

Touraine, A. (1990). The Idea of Revolution. In M. Featherstone (Ed.). *Global Culture: Nationalism, globalization and modernity* (pp. 121-142). London: Sage Publications.

Vervoorn, A. (1998). Globalisation and insulation in Asia. *Reorient* (pp. 1-19). Melbourne: Oxford University Press.

Vidich, A. & Lyman, S. (1994). Qualitative Methods: Their history in sociology and anthropology. In N. Denzin & Y. Lincoln (Eds.). *Handbood of Qualitative Research* (pp. 175-188). Thousand Oaks CA: Sage Publications.

Vogel, E.F. & Bell, N.W. (1968). The emotionally disturbed child as the family scapegoat. In N.W. Bell & E.G. Vogel (Eds.). *A Modern Introduction to the* Family (pp. 412-427). New York: Free Press.

Wallace, W. (1995). Rescue or Retreat? The Nation State in Western Europe, 1945-93. In J. Dunn, *Contemporary Crisis of the Nation State* (pp. 52-76). Oxford: Blackwell.

Wallerstein, I. (1991). *Geopolitics and Geoculture: Essays on the changing world-system.* Cambridge: Polity Press.

Warner, R. (1985). *Recovery from Schizophrenia: Psychiatry and political economy.* London: Routledge & Kegan Paul.

Waters, M. (1995). *Globalization.* London: Routledge.

Watzlawick, P., Beavin, J. & Jackson, D. (1967). *Pragmatics of Human Communication: A study of interactional patterns, pathologies, and paradoxes.* New York: Norton.

Weakland, J. (1976). The "Double Bind" Hypothesis of Schizophrenia and Three-Party Interaction. In C. Sluzki & D. Ransom. (Eds.). *Double Bind: The foundation of the communicational approach to the family* (pp. 23-38). New York: Grune & Stratton.

Webster, F. (1995). *Theories of The Information Society.* London: Routledge.

Weiner, N. (1954). *The Human Use of Human Beings.* London: Eyre & Spottiswood.

Weiner, N. (1968). *Cybernetics.* New York: John Wiley & Sons.

Wilden, A. (1975). Piaget and the Structure as Law and Order. In K.F. Riegel & G.C. Rosenwald (Eds.). *Structure and Transformation* (pp. 83-118). New York: John Riley & Sons.

Wilden, A. & Wilson, T. (1976). The double bind: Logic, magic and economic. In C. Sluzki & D. Ransom (Eds.). *Double Bind: The foundation of the communications approach to the family* (pp. 263-286). New York: Gryne & Stratton.

Wilden, A. (1978a). Ecology and Ideology. In A. Idris-Soven, E. Idris-Soven & M. Vaughan (Eds.). *The World as a Company Town* (pp. 73-78). The Hague: Mouton Publishers.

Wilden, A. (1978b). Ecosystems and Economic Systems. In M. Maruyama & A. Harkins (Eds.). *Cultures of the Future* (pp. 101-124). The Hague: Mouton Publishers.

Wilden, A. (1980) *System and Structure: Essays in communication and exchange* (2nd ed.). London: Tavistock.

Wilden, A. (1981). Semiotics as praxis: Strategy and tactics. *Recherches Semiotiques/Semiotic Inquiry,* 1, 1-34.

Wilden, A. (1987). *The Rules Are No Game: The strategy of communication.* London: Routledge & Kegan Paul.

Wiseman, J. (1998). *Global Nation? Australia and the politics of globalisation.* Cambridge: Cambridge University Press.

Young, I. (1984). Is male genderidentity the cause of male domination? In J. Trebilcot (Ed.). *Mothering: Essays on feminist theory* (pp. 129-146). Totawa NJ: Rowman & Allenheld.

Young, M. & Willmott, P. (1962). *Family and Kinship in East London* (Rev. ed.). Harmondsworth: Penguin Books.

Young, M. & Willmott, P. (1973). *The Symmetrical Family.* Harmondsworth: Penguin Books.

Zaretsky, E. (1976). *Capitalism, the Family and Personal Life.* London: Pluto Press.

Zelditch, M. (1955). Role Differentiation in the Nuclear Family: A comparative study. In T. Parsons & R. Bales (in collaboration with J. Olds, M. Zelditch & P. Slater), *Family, Socialization and Interaction Process* (pp. 307-352). Glencoe, Illinois: The Free Press of Glencoe.

Zorbaugh, H. (1929). *The Gold Coast and the Slum: A sociological study of Chicago's near north side.* Chicago: University of Chicago Press.

INDEX